THE CREATE-IT KIT

By Kim Baker & Sunny Baker
Illustrated by John Wincek

RANDOM HOUSE
ELECTRONIC PUBLISHING

Table of Contents

1. BE CREATIVE IN PRINT—BECOME A DESKTOP PUBLISHER!

This book will get you into print! It shows you how to make signs, flyers, birthday cards, newspapers, and much more. In fact, with the help of the software included with the book and a computer, you can create almost anything that can be printed. You could even write and print your own book like this one!

When people use a personal computer to create

publications like cards, books, and flyers it's called *desktop publishing*. After creating the projects in this book, you'll be a real desktop publisher, just like the people who create the cards, magazines, and newspapers you can buy at a store.

In the back of the book is an envelope with a computer disk in it. The disk contains a powerful desktop publishing program called EnVision Publisher. You will use EnVision Publisher and your computer to put words and pictures together to create all kinds of printed projects. Just follow the steps in the book.

The disk includes more than fifty fun pictures, too! You can use these pictures in any of your publications. There is also an order form at the back of the book so you can get another disk with pictures to create even more publications.

MEET BIT AND BYTE—YOUR CREATIVE MOUSE FRIENDS

These two mice will show you how to become a desktop publisher!

And this is Byte

This is Bit

You will see Bit and Byte throughout the book. Bit, Byte, and their many mouse friends will show you everything you need to know to make all sorts of publications. They will also give you ideas for doing lots of other creative things. But, before you and your new mouse friends get started, you need to learn a few things about publishing—and you'll need install the EnVision Publisher program on the computer.

LOAD ENVISION AND GET STARTED!

With the help of an adult who knows about the computer you'll be using, follow the directions on page 215. It takes only three to seven minutes to install EnVision on most computers. While your adult helper is doing this, you can read this chapter to learn how publishing was done before computers were invented. Once you see how much work publishing used to be, you will see why desktop publishing is so important—and why it's so much fun!

WRITING CAME FIRST, THEN CAME PUBLISHING!

Before people could publish anything, they had to invent writing. It took several thousand years to develop writing. Before writing, people used pictures instead of letters. Each picture told a story. The pictures took a long time to draw, so it took a long time to get a message across.

Over time, the pictures became symbols and it took less time to write a message. These symbols were called pictographs. These pictographs are much different from the A B Cs you know because each pictograph stood for one word. A picture of a dog meant dog. A picture of rain meant rain.

The ancient Egyptians invented some of the most interesting pictographs, called hieroglyphics. Thousands of years ago, the Egyptians wrote messages inside the pyramids with hieroglyphics. Eventually, they began writing hieroglyphics on long rolls of primitive paper made with papyrus, a reed-like plant that grows in Egypt. They called these long documents scrolls. Here are some examples of very old Egyptian hieroglyphics.

As you can see, these symbols are really little pictures.

Imagine how long it would take to write a letter if you had to use an alphabet like this!

The first writing used pictures called pictographs.

Eventually, people figured out that they could use a symbol to represent a sound. These symbols, which are called letters, make up the alphabet. Different alphabets were invented in different countries—but they all work in a similar way. The symbols represent sounds. When the symbols are combined, they make words. Alphabets made writing faster and easier than using pictures for everything. More than two thousand years ago, the ancient Romans invented an alphabet similar to the one you use today.

Copying books and scrolls by hand was a long, slow, and dull process.

With an alphabet of letters, long messages could be written on paper, and stories could be made into books. Anyone who knew the alphabet could learn to read. New words could be added to the vocabulary by combining the letters. This meant that more words could be used in the messages.

Even with the new alphabets, however, there was a major problem. Every book and document had to be written by hand. Even hundreds of years after the invention of the alphabet, people in Europe labored over tables copying important books by hand with pen and ink.

Making a single copy of the Bible took more than a year. There had to be a better way to make copies...

The Bible was the most important book of the time. Because the Bible took so long to copy, there were only a few copies to go around. Most people couldn't read because there were so few books to learn from. This got people thinking of better ways to copy books. These smart people invented printing.

AT LAST, PRINTING WAS INVENTED!

People figured out that they could carve words into wood panels so they could make more copies of books. These carved panels were called *printing plates*. Each wood plate contained a single page. To make a copy of the page, the plate was rubbed with ink and pressed hard

The first printing was done by carving the words of each page into a piece of wood. Printing this way was faster than copying by hand, but the carved plates wore out quickly.

against a piece of paper with a special machine called a *printing press.* It was no longer necessary to copy each letter, word, and page of a book by hand. The wood panel printing method reduced the time it took to create a Bible from about a year to only a few days!

Though an improvement, this method of printing didn't work out that well over time. The carving of a wood plate could take days. And, unfortunately, the plates often broke after printing only a few copies of the book. A new plate had to be carved to replace a broken one. A mistake in carving meant throwing the entire plate away. If a word was spelled wrong, a new plate had to be carved to fix the error. There had to be an even better way to make copies of books.

THEY FINALLY GOT IT RIGHT

To solve the problem of printing with wood panels, some more smart people put their thinking caps on. Instead of carving a plate from one piece of wood, why not assemble a plate from individual wooden letters? Rather than carving words into a single piece of wood, they carved separate letters that could be put together to form the words. The letters could be switched around to fix a mistake.

For example, if Finally was accidentally spelled Fianlly the letters an could be moved around to fix the mistake instead of carving a whole new plate. If one or two letters on a page wore out, new letters could be made to replace the bad ones. More importantly, the individual wood letters could be reused to print other books.

The invention was called *movable type*, because the individual letters could be moved around to form any word and then used again to create words on another page.

A plate made from a single piece of wood had to be replaced if a single mistake was made in carving it.

THEY
FINALLY
GOT IT
RIGHT

THEY
FINALLY
GOT IT
RIGHT

Making a plate from separate letters allowed mistakes to be fixed. This allowed a single broken letter to be replaced instead of carving an entire new plate.

A curious mouse discovers electricity while testing movable type.

The movable letters were put together in a special holder called a *type chase*. When the type chase was full of words, it became the plate used to print the page on a printing press.

PUBLISHING GETS EASIER AND FASTER

The first printing presses were made from the same machines used to press olives to make oil. They could only print one piece of paper at a time and were very slow. Over time, the printing presses became bigger, faster, and more precise. Today, the large printing presses used by newspapers and book publishers can print more than 100,000 pieces of paper in an hour.

Movable type changed too. Because wooden letters took a long time to carve, people invented a process known as *typefounding* that allowed type to be molded from metal instead of carved from wood. Because hot, molten metal was used to make the letters, the type was called *hot type*.

A German man, Johannes Gutenberg, is credited with the invention of hot type in the year 1455 A.D. (over 450 years ago). Many people believe that people in China may have invented the process much earlier.

Typefounding and hot type made it much faster to produce the type for books and newspapers. With this invention, more books became available and almost everyone learned to read.

About fifty years ago hot type was replaced with *cold type* produced from electronic typesetting machines. The cold type was produced photographically on paper and then used to make printing plates on metal with special chemicals.

The biggest change in publishing came about only a few years ago when small computers like the one you use were able to produce complete pages ready for printing on a printing press.

DESKTOP PUBLISHING IS BORN!

In 1985, a man named Paul Brainard came up with the phrase *desktop publishing*. He used this term to describe publishing and printing done with computers small enough to fit on a desk. Paul started a company that makes a famous desktop publishing program called PageMaker. Other people developed desktop publishing programs for personal computers as well. In addition to PageMaker, some of the other popular desktop publishing programs are QuarkXPress, Ready-Set-Go, and Ventura Publisher.

Desktop publishing programs contain the instructions that the computer uses to make pages for books and other publications. The program you will learn to use, EnVision Publisher, does most of the same things as PageMaker and other desktop publishing programs.

MAKE YOURSELF PART OF HISTORY—START PUBLISHING TODAY!

Desktop publishing is very important because it is a faster, easier way to produce books and other printed things. Today, even the large machines once used to produce the type for newspapers and magazines are being replaced by small computers just like yours. With EnVision Publisher and a computer you can do all the things real publishers do, such as setting type, adding designs and pictures to your publications, and making copies on the printer.

Once you learn these skills, you can call yourself a desktop publisher. In fact, you'll be able to print out a special certificate to hang on your wall that will prove your creative skills to everyone. (You'll learn how to make the certificate in the last chapter of the book.)

When you become a desktop publisher, an exciting adventure awaits you. You can influence the world with your words. You can make people happy with your gift of cards. You can inform people of special

Modern desktop publishers set type on their computers while sitting in a comfortable chair.

events with your signs and flyers. You can report the news in your own newspaper. These achievements will make you an important part of the history of publishing.

Are you ready to get started? If you are, just keep reading. Hundreds of wonderful publications are just waiting to be created!

2. MOUSE AROUND WITH YOUR COMPUTER—LEARN ABOUT ENVISION PUBLISHER

Bet you can't wait to become a desktop publisher! Bring this book and sit down in front of your computer. Turn your computer on. After flipping the switch, you'll see your computer wake up. A computer needs only about 15 to 30 seconds to wake up. That's probably less

Your computer wakes up when you turn it on.

time than it takes you to get out of bed! You will see a bunch of words fly by on the screen as the computer awakes and readies itself for work.

Once your computer is ready, you can start EnVision Publisher. You'll learn how to do that soon. But first, it's time to learn about the different parts of the computer. If you are already a computer genius, you already know how the computer works—so go to page 21 where it says "Starting EnVision Publisher." But, if you are just learning how to use a computer, read on.

WHAT ARE ALL THOSE BOXES WITH THE PLUGS AND WIRES?

Your computer is made up of several parts. The main box of your computer contains the CPU, which stands for *central processing unit.* The CPU is the brains of the outfit. It tells the other parts of the computer what to do and when to do it. The brain in your computer isn't really very smart, though. It's not nearly as smart as you. It's not even as smart as a dog or cat. In fact, it's really pretty dumb. Even a goldfish is smarter than a computer. But, the brain in a computer is good for one thing—it can quickly follow any number of step-by-step instructions. You can tell a computer to add 2+2 a hundred times if you want to, or even a million times. It will do it instantly. Computers never get bored. Even if

With EnVision Publisher installed, your computer is a complete publishing system.

The monitor is like a television that lets you see what your computer is doing.

The CPU, the brains of your computer, is in this box. This box is also where the computer stores things on disks.

The keyboard is used to type words into the computer and to tell it what to do.

The mouse is used to draw and to control things.

Dot-matrix printer or ink-jet printer

Your computer may have a dot-matrix, ink-jet, or laser printer. Laser printers use a real laser to "draw" the image on the printed page. Dot-matrix printers use dots to make letters and shapes. Ink-jet printers use special "pens" to draw images. Some printers will print on rolls of paper. Other printers print on single sheets of paper. Any of these printers will work with EnVision Publisher.

Laser printer

they aren't very bright, computers are handy tools that work very fast and rarely make mistakes.

Computers need humans like you to tell them what to do. It's the instructions that people write for computers that make them *seem* smart. These instructions are called *programs*. EnVision Publisher is one of many programs that you can use to tell the CPU in your computer system how to do things you want to do.

FLOPPY DISKS AND THE HARD DISK

The main box of your computer has slots where you put *floppy disks*. Most computers have two slots for floppy disks. One slot is for big disks and one is for small disks. The big slot is usually called the A disk drive and the small slot is called the B disk drive.

You use floppy disks to save work you create with the computer. Floppy disks work something like cassette tapes that record and play music or video cassettes that record and play movies and TV shows. The computer records information on the disks and can play the information back from the disk.

There is another kind of disk drive built into your computer that you can't see from the outside. It's called a *hard disk* and it's where EnVision Publisher is kept once you install it on your machine. The hard disk holds much more information than a floppy disk. It can't be taken out of the machine. The hard disk is usually called the C disk drive.

THE MONITOR SHOWS YOU WHAT'S GOING ON

To see what the CPU is doing, you need a monitor. This is the box that looks like a television with no volume control or tuning buttons. You can't watch TV shows on most computer monitors, but you can see what the computer is doing.

THE KEYBOARD LETS YOU TYPE THINGS IN

The keyboard is used to control the computer and to type words and commands.

THE MOUSE LETS YOU POINT TO THINGS

Your computer also uses a mouse that is moved around on your desk to control the computer.

You can use EnVision Publisher without a mouse, but it's much easier to use with one.

THE PRINTER MAKES THE OUTPUT

To print your publications, you'll use your computer's printer. When you instruct your computer to print, the CPU tells the printer "Wake up, too!" The CPU then sends the words and information to the printer, which then sets to work printing. Once all the printing is complete, the CPU tells the printer to go back to sleep until it's needed again. (Of course, you have to make sure that the printer is plugged in and turned on.)

EVERYTHING WORKS TOGETHER

The computer, monitor, keyboard, mouse, and printer are connected with wires. The CPU sends messages over these wires to control the other parts of the computer. The keyboard and mouse are wired to the computer, too, so you can give the computer instructions with the help of the EnVision Publisher program. Together, these parts work as one unit to allow you to create and print your publication!

STARTING ENVISION PUBLISHER

It's time to get EnVision Publisher ready for publishing. If you've never used the computer before, you'll probably want to work through the following steps with an adult or a friend who knows how to use the computer.

With your computer already turned on and awake, you should see a C> on the screen. If you do, then you're

ready to start EnVision Publisher! (If you see the words "Program Manager" at the top of your screen, skip to "Does Your Machine Use Windows?" on page 24.)

In Case You Forgot...
If EnVision has not been installed on your computer, it's time to do it now. Work with an adult or someone who knows about your computer, and follow the easy instructions on page 215.

HOW TO START ENVISION PUBLISHER

Step 1.   When you see the symbol C> on your computer monitor, type CD EVP and press Enter on the keyboard to go to the place EnVision Publisher is kept on the hard disk.

Step 2.   Now, type EVP and press Enter to start the program. If you have done this correctly, the words EnVision Publisher will appear on the screen in a few seconds. Sit back and watch while the computer thinks about things.

The EnVision Publisher words will disappear in a few seconds. Then you'll see something that looks like the picture on the next page. This means EnVision Publisher is ready and waiting to create something with you.

| File | Edit | Page | Text | Options | Help | | | | | | | UN |

| READY | Helvetic |
| View all |
| ✓ 100% size |
| 200% size |
| 400% size |
| Go to... |
| Insert... |
| Delete... |
| Clear |
| Setup... |
| Left master |
| Right master |

EnVision Publisher is ready to go to work!

On the screen you can see the controls for EnVision Publisher and part of a blank page. The controls are used to tell EnVision how to do things. The blank page is where you will create your publications. Before you can make something, however, you need to learn a little bit about the controls and buttons you see on the screen.

Hold the mouse straight as you move it. The pointer on the screen will move as you move the mouse. Try it!

23

DOES YOUR MACHINE USE WINDOWS SOFTWARE?

If your machine uses a program called Microsoft Windows, you'll need to start EnVision Publisher a different way. If you see the words Program Manager at the top of your computer's screen, here's how to close Windows and run EnVision Publisher:

Step 1. Click twice quickly with your mouse on the small box at the far upper left corner of the monitor. If nothing happens, double click again.

Click here in → the little box!

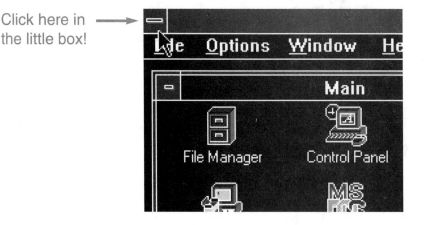

Step 2. An Information Box opens on screen. It asks you whether you want to end your Windows session. Click once on the OK button.

Step 3. Type CD\EVP\EVP. This will move you to where EnVision is kept and will start the program. Make sure you type these letters exactly or it won't work. Use the slash symbol (\) located just over the Enter Key. Don't use the one next to the Shift Key because it won't work. (If you see the message Invalid Directory or Bad command or file name, try typing CD..\EVP\EVP. If that doesn't work either, the program may be kept in a different place on your computer's hard disk. Ask an adult to help you find it.)

MOUSING AROUND

The first thing you need to know to make EnVision work is how to use a mouse. The mouse moves the pointer you see on your monitor screen. When you move the mouse, the pointer moves.

A mouse on his pad

GET YOURSELF A MOUSE PAD!

You'll want a mouse pad to put under your mouse. A mouse pad makes it easier to move the mouse around. Mouse pads are available from computer stores or you can make your own. Just put an ordinary magazine under your mouse. Try different magazines until you find one that lets the mouse move smoothly.

☞ Go ahead! Try it. Move the mouse around on the mouse pad and see what happens. The best way to move the mouse is to keep the mouse straight as you move it, as shown in the picture. That makes it easier to move the pointer exactly where you want it.

MOUSE BUTTONS

Most mouses have two buttons, and some mouses have three buttons on them. (Yes, the plural of the animal mouse is mice, but the plural of the computer mouse is mouses.) In this book, you'll mostly use the left button. Only use the right mouse button if the book tells you to do so. (If you have a three-button mouse, use the left and right buttons. Don't use the middle button.)

When you click on the mouse button, it makes things happen. First, you'll use the mouse to move the pointer where you want it on your screen; then, you'll click to make something happen. Sometimes you need to click once. Other times you need to click twice. When you click twice it's called a double click.

Until you get the hang of it, the book will tell you what button to use and whether to click once or double click. Remember that a double click is two clicks done very quickly. You may want to practice double clicking until you can do it in less than a second without moving the mouse.

TAKE A TOUR OF ENVISION PUBLISHER

Now that you know how to move the mouse, you're ready to learn about EnVision Publisher. Fasten your seatbelt because you're going to take a fast tour of EnVision and its tools. Once you complete the tour, you can go on to the next chapter and create your first publication—a cool sign to hang on the door to your room.

When you first start EnVision, you will see the screen shown here. You will see three sets of controls that you use to tell EnVision what to do: the pull-down menus, the Toolbar, and the Control Bar. You don't need to learn how to use the controls right now. You only need to locate them.

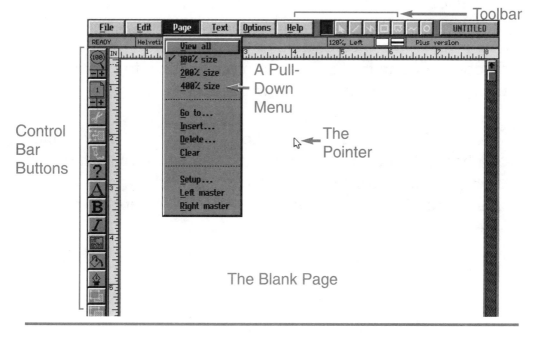

PULLING DOWN ON THE PULL-DOWN MENUS

The six buttons at the top, left side of the screen control the pull-down menus. Pull-down menus appear on screen when you click on their buttons. By clicking once on the button, a list of commands pops up. (Commands tell the computer what to do.) Try it with your mouse. Here are the steps.

DO IT   HOW TO USE THE PULL-DOWN MENUS

Step 1.   Click once with the left button of your mouse on the button for the pull-down menu named File. See what happens? A list of commands pops up instantly! You can choose one of these commands by clicking on it. But for now, you don't need to try that. Just remember how to click on the button to pull down the pull-down menus!

Step 2.   Pull-down menus disappear from the screen after you choose one of the commands. Another way to make a pull-down menu disappear is to click anywhere else on the screen. Zap! The menu disappears. Try it. Click in the middle of the page to zap the menu.

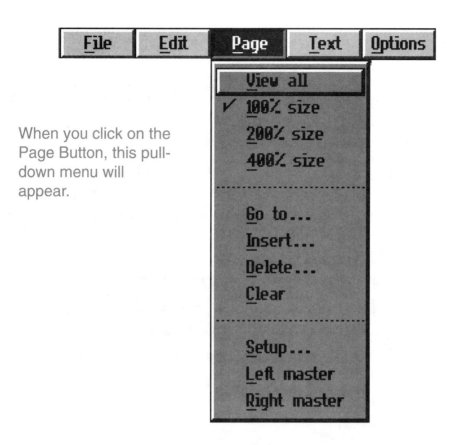

When you click on the Page Button, this pull-down menu will appear.

GRAB A TOOL FROM THE TOOLBAR

The EnVision Publisher Toolbar is located at the right side of the top of the screen. These tools are used for drawing and working with words. You select a tool by clicking on it once with your mouse. Try it. The steps are explained on the next page.

DO IT HOW TO CHOOSE A TOOL FROM THE TOOLBAR

Step 1. Click once on any tool, as shown below. Once you click, it looks like you pushed a button!

Step 2. To select another tool, just click on another button. The button for the first tool you click on will pop up again. Go ahead. Click the tools on and off as many times as you want.

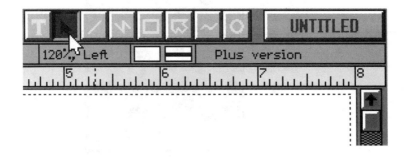

CONTROLLING THE CONTROL BAR

The third set of controls is the Control Bar at the left edge of the screen. The Control Bar is used for changing the way words look, printing your work, and other useful things. It works like the Toolbar. You just click once on the buttons to choose them. Try it now. Click on the ? button. This brings up an information box that tells you how

EnVision works. This box is called the Help information box. Put it away by clicking on the Cancel button in the box and it will disappear. You can click on any of the buttons on the Control Bar. Go ahead. It won't hurt anything.

Try it. Click on the buttons on the Toolbar and see what you find.

INFORMATION BOXES

When you use the buttons and commands in EnVision, other information boxes may appear. These boxes tell you when EnVision needs an answer to a question. Just answer the question in the box, and EnVision will follow your command.

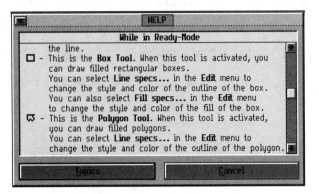

The Help Information Box appears when you click on the ? button on the Control Bar.

THE BLANK PAGE

In addition to EnVision's controls, there is a place on the screen where you do all your work. It is called the blank page. This is where you will type and draw to create publications. The blank page is like a blank piece of paper. You can add things to it, draw on it, or erase what you've added with an electronic eraser.

Now you know how the three kinds of EnVision controls work. It's time to check out some of the tools and buttons to see what they do.

TYPE WORDS WITH THE TEXT TOOL

Almost all your publications will use words, so the first thing to try is a little typing. If your typing skills are weak, the computer will wait patiently while you hunt and peck for each letter. You don't have to worry about going fast. Just type at your own pace. If you mess something up, don't worry. You can fix almost any mistake you make with EnVision. Just read how to fix mistakes on the next page. It's easy! Now, follow these steps to type your name on the blank page.

HOW TO TYPE WORDS WITH ENVISION

Step 1. Single click on the Text Tool to select it. It's the tool with the T on it. Now EnVision is almost ready for you to type your name using the keyboard.

Type your words using the Text Tool!

Step 2. You need to tell EnVision where to type your name. To do this, click once anywhere on the blank page. Once you do this, you will see a flashing line (|) on the blank page. This flashing line is called a *cursor* and it means EnVision is ready for you to type something.

Step 3. Type your name using the keyboard. As you type each letter, it will appear on the page on your monitor.

Made a Mistake? Not you...

To fix mistakes when typing your name, just use the Backspace *key to back up and erase your typing. After you back up over the error, type the correction and the rest of your name. You can do this as many times as necessary. Just keep trying until you get it right.*

That's it! You've set your first piece of type using a computer. This is just how typesetting is done in modern publishing companies and newspapers. You have to admit that it's a whole lot easier than carving your name into a piece of wood to make a press plate for printing!

MAKING TEXT BOXES TO PUT WORDS WHERE YOU WANT THEM

You just learned how to type in words with the Text Tool, but you can also use the Text Tool to show EnVision where you want to put the type (words) on the blank page. That's right, you must tell EnVision where on the page you want the text to appear. To do this, you need to draw a text box with the Text Tool. Otherwise, there's no way to enter words on the page.

Wait a minute! Are you wondering how come you were able to type in your name just a minute ago? What's going on?

That's a good question. If you need a thing called a text box to type in words, how did you just type your name without drawing a text box? Easy. Sneaky too.

EnVision thinks you will probably want to start your publications by typing as soon as you start the program. To make things simple, when you start the program, EnVision draws a BIG text box for you on the blank page (so it's not entirely blank after all). You are really typing into a box that's already there. You can see the dotted outline of the text box on your screen, as shown in the next picture.

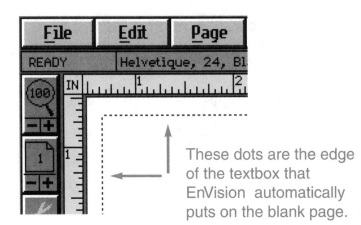

These dots are the edge of the textbox that EnVision automatically puts on the blank page.

Later in the book you'll learn how to draw your own text boxes for placing words exactly where you want them on a page. For now, just use the text box that EnVision puts there for you.

THE BOX TOOL DRAWS SQUARES AND RECTANGLES

EnVision has lots of tools for drawing. One of them is the Box Tool. You probably guessed it already. The Box Tool is for drawing squares and rectangles of all sizes. You can use the boxes you draw as shapes and

borders around words. EnVision Publisher also lets you fill boxes with color. You'll learn how to do that later in the book. For now, try these steps to draw a box.

HOW TO DRAW A BOX

Step 1. Click on the Box Tool. That's the tool with the picture of a square on it.

Step 2. Pick a place on the blank page where you want to start your box. The upper left corner of the blank page is a good place to start your first box.

Step 3. Hold down the mouse button. Move the mouse toward the bottom of the screen while holding the button down. You'll see the lines of the top of the box moving as you move your mouse. When you hold down the mouse button while moving the mouse, it is called dragging the mouse. You'll use this skill often in desktop publishing. As you drag, you'll see a box appear on the screen.

Step 4. Stop dragging when your box is big enough. A box about two inches square should be the right size.

Step 5. Click on the Pointer Tool to tell EnVision you're done drawing the box. The Pointer Tool is the button with the arrow on it in the Toolbox. Once you click, you'll see your finished box! Easy, isn't it? Draw some more boxes on the page if you want to.

THE CIRCLE TOOL MAKES CIRCLES AND OVALS

The Circle Tool works just like the Box Tool, except it draws circles and ovals, not boxes. But since it works just the same, try drawing an oval by following the steps for the Box Tool; But, don't click on the Box Tool; instead, click on the Circle Tool. Drag to draw a circle, just like you did to draw the box. (Remember how to drag? Click on the mouse button and hold it down while moving the mouse.) Draw your circle next to the first box. Make it about the same size. Don't forget to select the Pointer Tool after you draw the circle so you can see it better on your monitor.

THE LINE TOOL DRAWS LINES

Okay, you guessed it again! The Line Tool draws lines. It works very much like the Box Tool and the Circle Tool. Try drawing a line under the box and the circle following the same steps. Just click on the Line Tool and drag. Remember to click on the Pointer Tool after you draw the line so you can see it better on the screen.

YOUR MONITOR SHOULD LOOK SOMETHING LIKE THIS!

You've now used three tools in EnVision's Toolbar to draw boxes, circles, and lines. Your page might look something like the one below. It doesn't matter if the shapes you drew are bigger, smaller, or in different places on the page. Just have fun and draw what you want.

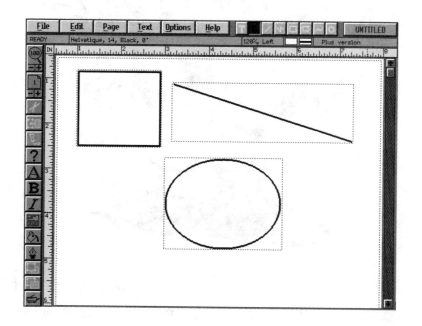

MOVING THINGS WITH THE POINTER TOOL

You've already used the Pointer Tool to make your boxes, circles, and lines more visible. The Pointer Tool can do other useful things, too.

The Pointer Tool can move things around on the page. It can also make things bigger or smaller.

Remember that the Pointer Tool is the button that looks like an arrow on the Toolbar. To move something around on the page, just try the steps that follow.

DO IT HOW TO MOVE THINGS WITH THE POINTER TOOL

Step 1. Click on the Pointer Tool in the Toolbar.

Step 2. Click once on one of the shapes you just drew. It doesn't matter if it is a box, circle, or line. One click will select the shape. When you select the shape, that tells EnVision that you want to do something to it. Several small black squares will appear at the corners.

Step 3. Move the pointer to one of the black squares. See how the pointer becomes a target? Click on the black square *but don't release the mouse button.*

Step 4. Now, drag the square. What happens? The shape

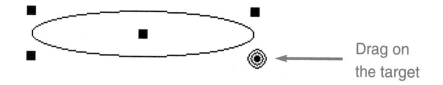

Drag on
the target

changes shape as shown on the next page! As you drag the black square, the shape becomes bigger or smaller depending on how you move the square. Try it again on another shape. Experiment by making all the objects bigger and smaller on the page.

Step 5. Now click down on the middle square in an object. Hold down on the mouse button, and a hand

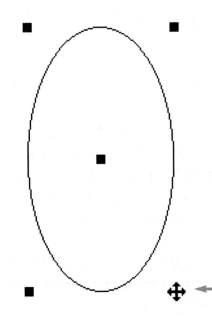

When you click and
drag on the squares
you can change the
size and shape of
the circle.

will appear. This lets you drag the object around on the
page. Try it. Move things all around on the page.

GETTING RID OF THINGS WITH THE POINTER TOOL

Now that you know how to draw and move boxes,
circles, and lines, the blank page is starting to look a little
cluttered, to say the least. Luckily, the Pointer Tool also can
be used to erase boxes and other shapes from the page.

It's time to get rid of this stuff so you can try out other
tools in the Toolbox. Follow the steps on the next page to
delete objects with the Pointer Tool.

HOW TO DELETE OBJECTS

Step 1. To delete the circle, click on it once with the Pointer Tool. This selects it.

Step 2. Press the Delete key or Backspace key on your keyboard. An information box will appear asking if you really want to delete the box.

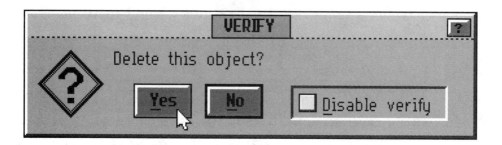

Step 3. Click the Yes button once with your mouse. This will put the information box away and erase the circle completely.

Repeat the same steps to delete the box and then the line. Delete all the objects.

Once you've cleared the page, it's time to try out more of EnVision's amazing drawing tools.

THE AMAZING POLYGON, SQUIGGLE, AND ZIGZAG TOOLS

Sometimes you need to draw more complicated things. A box, line, or circle just won't do. No problem, because EnVision Publisher provides more tools for drawing. There's a Polygon Tool that lets you draw boxes with as many sides as you want, a Zigzag Tool that allows you to draw crooked lines, and a Squiggle Tool that draws weird curved lines.

The three tools work in similar ways. The Zigzag and the Squiggle Tool let you draw fun, wavy lines. The Squiggle Tool converts your slightly shaky lines into perfect curves. You have to try it to understand how it works, because it's wild! But, enough talk. It's time for you to try these tools out. Here's what to do.

Waves are like squiggles.

DO IT HOW TO DRAW POLYGONS, ZIGZAGS, AND SQUIGGLES

Step 1. Choose a tool by clicking on it once. The Polygon Tool has a weird-looking square on it. The Zigzag Tool looks like a zigzag line, and the Squiggle Tool has a squiggly line on it.

Step 2. Click once to start the line. Then move the mouse to create a line and click again. You don't need to drag because the line will follow the mouse automatically.

Step 3. Keep moving the mouse and clicking as you go. You can create as many lines in as many directions as you want.

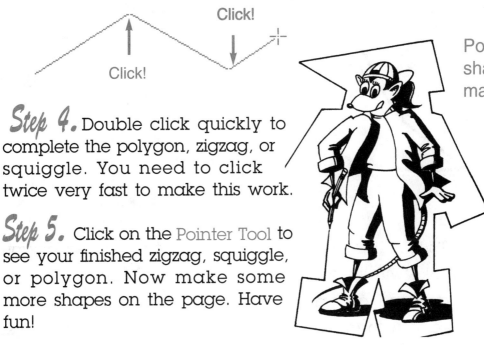

Click!

Click!

Polygons are shapes with many sides.

Step 4. Double click quickly to complete the polygon, zigzag, or squiggle. You need to click twice very fast to make this work.

Step 5. Click on the Pointer Tool to see your finished zigzag, squiggle, or polygon. Now make some more shapes on the page. Have fun!

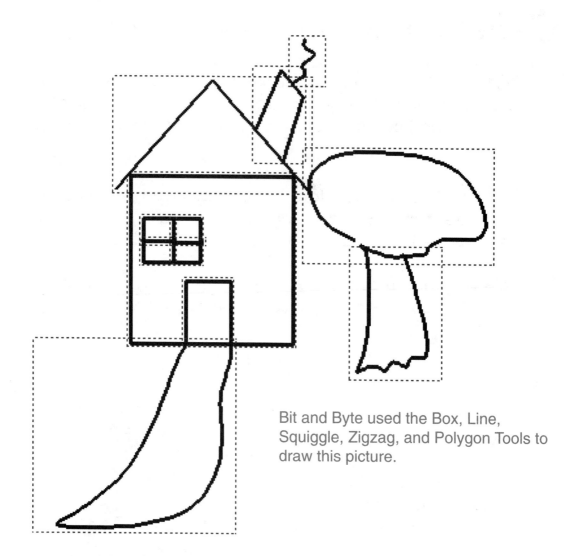

Bit and Byte used the Box, Line, Squiggle, Zigzag, and Polygon Tools to draw this picture.

That's all there is to it! Just think of the drawings you can make with these cool tools! You can use them to create shapes such as arrows, pictures like a house, or a landscape with mountains and hills. You can create almost any shape, no matter how unusual, by mixing different shapes on the page.

PRINT YOUR SQUIGGLES!

Publishing isn't much fun if you can't print your creations. To print what you just drew, have an adult read the information on page 221 to set up your computer's printer.

If your printer is ON and has been set up correctly, all you need to do is click on the Printer Button in the Control Panel, as shown. This brings up the Printer Control Box.

Click once here to print →

Click OK in this box and your publication will be printed on your printer. That's all there is to it!

QUITTING TIME

Try out everything as much as you want. Use the tools to draw pictures. Type in words. Print the results. But, even though you're having fun, at some point you'll want to turn EnVision Publisher off for the day. Here's how to finish up your session with EnVision Publisher. To quit, you use a command in one of the pull-down menus. Here are the steps.

DO IT

HOW TO TURN ENVISION PUBLISHER OFF

Step 1. Click once on the Pointer Tool and then click anywhere on the page where it's still blank. Don't click on a shape you've drawn or on the text box with your name in it. The idea is to make sure that nothing on the page is selected.

Step 2. Click once on the File button for the File pull-down menu. The menu should appear under the button instantly.

Step 3. In the list of commands, choose Exit at the bottom of the menu.

Step 4. An information box appears asking whether you

want to save your work. Click the No button once with your mouse.

In the next chapter you'll learn how to save your work, but since you were just mousing around today, you don't need to at this point.

The screen clears and the C> appears again, like it did before you started EnVision Publisher.

Step 5. Turn off your computer and head to the kitchen for a cool drink. You've earned it!

That's it for now. You've completed your introductory tour of EnVision Publisher. In the next chapter, you will create your first real publication. Get ready. Get set... Turn the page!

3. HAVE FUN WITH WORDS— CREATE YOUR OWN SIGNS

Signs, signs everywhere. Stop signs. Street signs. BIG SIGNS. Small signs. Even more signs. Signs on the walls. Signs on doors. Signs on your school. Signs on stores. Why do we need so many signs?

Every sign has a purpose. Danger signs protect us. Traffic signs direct us. Store signs show us where to buy things. Other signs help us find things.

THE WORDS ON SIGNS ARE IMPORTANT

Signs have been used by people for a long time. In fact, signs were even used when people lived in caves almost a million years ago—and that's a very, very long time before you were born. The first signs were painted on the walls of caves or on rocks. People didn't use words or letters on the cave signs because the alphabet hadn't been invented yet. Instead, they painted pictures to get their messages across. The paints they used were made from ground up berries, plants, and charcoal. The sign paintings showed people where to find water or how to locate food in the forest. Some of the sign paintings told stories.

Today, no matter where you live there are signs to inform you of things. People put signs almost anywhere—on poles, boards, and walls. People still use pictures in signs, but most signs depend on words. Signs are painted or printed in all sorts of shapes and sizes. The words used on signs are also written in different shapes and sizes.

When you go for a ride on your bike or in a car, look at the letters used on the signs you see. Notice the different shapes of the letters. The sign on your favorite toy store uses letters in lots of colors. The letters on your school sign are much different. On the grocery store the letters are also different. Think about it. It must be true that the shapes and sizes of the letters are important.

Here are some letters people can use on signs. All the letters below are still the letter A—but each one has a different shape.

A A A A A

Amazing! And look at this. All the letters below are the letter Z!

Z Z Z Z Z

Awesome! Why are there so many shapes for the letters? Why are the shapes and sizes of the letters important in signs and other printed things? To answer that question, consider your own handwriting for a moment and the handwriting of your friends, parents, and teacher.

For example, here is a sample of Sarah's handwriting.

This is a sample of Sarah's writing.

Here is a sample of Jason's writing.

This is a sample of Jason's writing.

See how Sarah's writing is slanted to the right. In each word, the letters are connected. Some of the letters have tails. Jason's handwriting slants to the left. Jason's letters have different shapes than Sarah's. Some of the letters in the words are not connected.

Your handwriting is unique too. Try it. Put a sample of your handwriting on the red line. If this isn't your own book, write a sample on another piece of paper.

Put your writing ⟶ here.

- -

Fantastic! Your handwriting is different than Sarah's and Jason's. You'll also discover that your handwriting is different than your best friend's. In fact, no one has handwriting exactly like you. And, as you get older, your writing will look different than it does now. That's because you will change and mature and your handwriting will change with you.

Even though most people learn to write letters the same way in school, everyone's handwriting is unique in some way. Do you know why people have handwriting that looks so different?

Right! Just like you, your writing has a special personality all its own. Handwriting is different because people are different. That's true of words used on signs and in other printed projects! The shape of the words on signs gives each message a unique and special personality.

A computer doesn't have a personality because it is a machine, but your EnVision program lets you give the words a personality. With EnVision, you can choose the way you want the alphabet to look when you type the words. Because the personality of the words you use is important on your signs and other printed projects, you will always need to decide how the words should look.

TYPEFACES HAVE PERSONALITIES TOO!

The many different shapes of the alphabets used by the computer are called *typefaces*. A typeface contains all of the capital letters from A to Z and all of the small letters from a to z. A typeface may also contain useful symbols.

For example, if you make a sign with a price on it, you can use a dollar symbol like this $ or a cents symbol like this ¢.

The people who create the different typefaces are called *type designers*. The type designers give the typefaces names. Some of the names given to typefaces are simple, like Times. Some are hard to say, like Helvetique. Some of the names are silly, like Thingamajigs. Here is an example of the typeface called Times. The Times typeface is often used in newspapers and books because it is easy to read.

ABCDEFHIJKLMNOPQRSTUVWXYZ

---

abcdefghijklmnopqrstuvwxyz

, . ? ! $ ¢ & % + - ; : " "

Just as your face looks different from everyone else's face, a typeface looks different from every other typeface. And just like your handwriting, the typefaces you use on your computer have different personalities. If you examine the different typefaces used in your books, on signs, in the newspaper, and on cards, you will soon notice the different personalities of the typefaces.

Some typefaces are strong.

I am a strong typeface called Franklin Gothic.

Some typefaces are funny.

I am a funny typeface called Dom Casual.

Some typefaces are very serious.

I am a serious typeface called Garamond.

Some typefaces are skinny and some are fat.

I am a thin typeface called Kabel Light.

I am a fat typeface called Bodoni Poster.

In the EnVision program you have eight typefaces you can use when you create your signs and other projects. On the next page you'll see samples of five of the typefaces you can use.

I am a typeface called Helvetique.

I am a typeface called Modern Stamp.

I am a typeface called Timeless.

I am a typeface called New Caligraph.

I AM A TYPEFACE CALLED SHADOW.

There is one typeface that you can use in EnVision that isn't letters at all. This typeface is called Dingbats. Dingbats is a typeface that uses symbols and pictures instead of letters. You can't read this typeface, but you might want to use it as a secret code with your friends. You can also use the symbols to decorate your projects or to create borders around pictures. When you use the Dingbat typeface, each letter on your keyboard will produce a symbol or picture instead of a letter.

Here are some symbols you can produce with the typeface called Dingbats.

When you are using EnVision, you can ask for a list of the typefaces. Here are the steps for you to try.

How to See the List of Typefaces

Step 1. Be sure you have started the EnVision program, as you did in the last chapter. Now, with your mouse, move the cursor to the letter A on the Control Bar.

Step 2. Click the letter A on the Control Bar. The box called Type Specs will pop up on your computer screen, as shown on the next page.

Here's the
list of
typefaces.

Click here
to open
the Type
Specs
box.

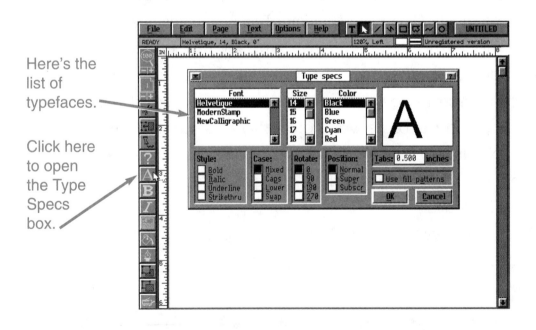

Step 3. To make the Type Specs list go away, use your mouse to point to the word Cancel.

Step 4. Click once on the word Cancel. The Type Specs list will disappear from the screen. Go ahead. Make the list appear and disappear on your screen.

CHOOSING A TYPEFACE FOR YOUR SIGN

When you make a sign or any other project with EnVision, you need to decide which typeface has the right personality for your message. If your message is serious, a typeface like Garamond would be a good choice. If your message is important, you might choose a big, bold typeface like Bodoni or Stencil.

Choosing a typeface with EnVision is easy! The steps below tell you how to do it.

How to Choose a Typeface

Step 1. Make the names of the typefaces appear as before by clicking on the A on the Control Bar.

Step 2. Move the cursor with your mouse to the name of the typeface you want to use. Click once on the name with your mouse. You will see the typeface you have selected appear in a box on the right-hand side.

Step 3. Try it. Choose different typefaces by clicking on the names. You will see the letters change in the box. It's fun, isn't it?

Step 4. Now choose a typeface and then click OK. The Type Specs box will disappear. When you click OK, it makes things happen. In this case, you've selected a typeface.

Step 5. Type your name using the keyboard. Your name will appear in the typeface you selected from the Type Specs box. Wow! Now try it again with another typeface. Just repeat the steps.

TYPEFACES CAN HAVE STYLES TOO!

After you decide on a typeface, there are other things you can do with EnVision to make the words look different. When you make a change to a typeface, it is called changing its style. Here are three important styles you can use in your signs and other projects.

You can make type lean on its side. When type leans over, it is called the *italic* style.

I am a sample of the Helvetica typeface in the italic style.

You can make a typeface much darker. This is called the **BOLD** style.

I am a sample of the Helvetica typeface in the bold style.

You can underline your words. This is called the <u>UNDERLINE</u> style.

<u>I am a sample of the Helvetica typeface in the underline style.</u>

To change the style of a typeface, you need to turn the styles On or Off. It's easy. Just follow these simple steps.

How to Change the Style of Your Text

DO IT

Step 1. While using EnVision, type your name in any typeface you want to use.

Step 2. Now, select your name by putting the cursor on your name with the mouse and then clicking twice very quickly. This will put a black box around your name. This is called *selecting text.* (If it doesn't work the first time, try clicking faster.)

Double click on the words to select them.

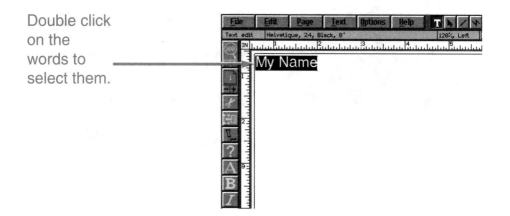

Step 3. With the text still selected, use the mouse to move the cursor to the TEXT menu and click on it. A menu will appear with many choices on it. The choices in the middle are the type styles including Bold, Italic, Underline, and other styles.

Step 4. Turn the style On by moving the cursor to that style. Click on the style until a check mark appears next to its name in the pull-down menu. To turn a style Off, click on it once more (with words selected) and this will remove the check mark. You can turn on more than one style at a time. Clicking on both Bold and Italic will add both styles to your type. You'll see a check mark appear next to each selected style.

A check mark shows next to each type style you select.

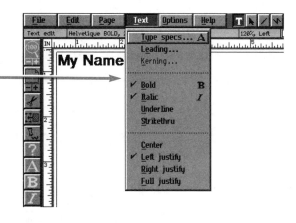

Step 5. After clicking on the style, the menu will go away, and the word you selected will be changed. Go ahead. Try it with all the styles. Choose some words. Then turn the styles On and turn the styles Off from the Text Menu. Like magic, the words change their appearance. It's a lot easier than trying to do this with a pen or brush, isn't it?

When you're done trying the different typefaces and turning the styles On and Off, you're ready to make your first sign. You can create signs for your room or make signs to take to school to announce a special event. There are hundreds of fun signs you can make for almost any reason you can imagine. Let's try it now.

NOW YOU CAN CREATE A SIGN. HERE ARE THE STEPS.

To make your first sign, just follow the steps below. When you're through, you'll have a cool sign that you can tape to the door of your bedroom or where you keep your computer. After you learn how to make this first sign, you can make as many signs as you want with your own words and ideas!

You will make your first sign the same size as a regular sheet of paper. Ordinary paper is 8 1/2 inches wide and 11 inches tall. First, you'll add words to make the sign using EnVision Publisher. Next, you'll add a box around the outside of the sign to make it look neater. Last, you can print your sign and glue it to a piece of cardboard or stiff paper to make it stronger and last longer. Here goes!

DO IT Create Your First Sign

Step 1. Start the EnVision program as you did before. If you can't remember how, look up the steps on page 21.

Step 2. Select the Text Tool and click on the blank page. When you make a sign, the first thing to do is type in the words. For this first sign, type the words shown below. (To make the first letter of a word a capital letter, hold down on the SHIFT Key when you type in the letter.) Don't worry about changing the typeface or style yet. You'll do that later. Just type in these words:

.

Creative Kid at Work, Please Knock

Step 3. Now, before you do anything else, you should name your sign and save it to disk. To do this, click on the File Button to display the pull-down menu. The menu will display 11 choices. Move to the choice called Save as... and click once on it. After clicking, the Save box will appear as shown below.

To give your sign a name, click in the File name box and hit the Backspace key to erase the old name. Type this name in the box:

SIGN1.EVP

Type the name of your sign in this box.

If you want to save your sign to a floppy disk, tell EnVision which one by clicking A: or B: here. Clicking on C: will save the sign on the hard disk.

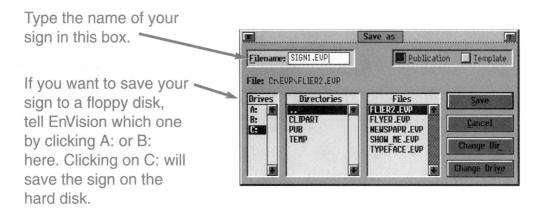

ENVISION USES SPECIAL NAMES FOR PUBLICATIONS

You may think that SIGN1.EVP is a strange name. When you name things in EnVision, you need to use special names that the computer can understand. What does this funny name mean to the computer? The SIGN1 is the name of your sign on the computer's disk. We called it SIGN1 because it is the first sign you will make. You can give it any name you want, but you can't use more than 8 letters in the name.

The .EVP at the end of the name tells EnVision Publisher that the sign was created with EnVision and not some other program. If you forget to add this .EVP ending, the computer will do it for you on the disk. .EVP will be the last name of all your EnVision projects stored on the disk in your computer. Important: The first name can have eight letters or fewer, but the last name is always .EVP, which is short for EnVision Publisher

After giving the sign a name, click on the SAVE button with your mouse to save the file to disk. If you want to save the file to a floppy disk, before clicking the Save button with your mouse, click on the correct letter for the floppy disk drive with your mouse. It will most likely be the letter A or B. (The hard disk is C.) Once you have named and saved your sign or other publication, it will always be available so you can print copies or make changes at a later date.

Earlier in this chapter you learned about typefaces. It's time to put that knowledge to work in your sign. In the next steps, you will make changes to the typeface to make the words look the way you want them to appear on the sign.

Step 4.   Select all the words in the sentence. Remember that you do this by moving the cursor to any letter in the sentence and then clicking twice, very quickly.

Step 5.   After the sentence is selected, move your cursor to the Text menu.This will cause the menu to drop. You will see the eleven choices you saw before. Click once on Center to center the words in the text box.

Step 1. Make sure the Text Tool is selected as shown. Clicking here will center the text.

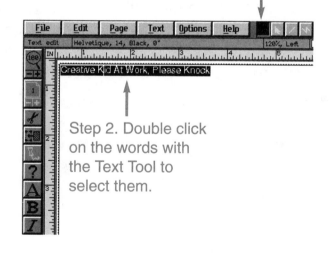

Step 2. Double click on the words with the Text Tool to select them.

Step 6.   Select the sentence again by clicking on it twice.

File	Edit	Page	**Text**	Options	Help

Text edit | Helvetique, 14, Bl |

Type specs... A
Leading...
Kerning...

Bold   **B**
Italic   *I*
Underline
Strikethru

Center
✓ Left justify
Right justify
Full justify

Creative Kid At W

Clicking on Center in the Text pull-down menu will
center the words within the big text box on the page.

Step 7.   Click once on the A in the Control Bar, as shown on the next page. This opens the Type Specs box you've seen before. In this box, you can choose a new typeface and make other changes to the words in your sign, such as making them bigger or smaller.

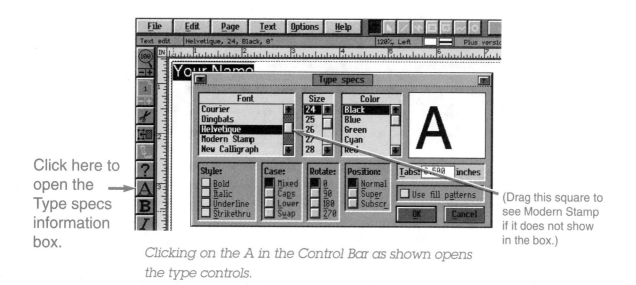

Click here to open the Type specs information box.

Clicking on the A in the Control Bar as shown opens the type controls.

(Drag this square to see Modern Stamp if it does not show in the box.)

Step 8.   This is supposed to be a COOL sign. The typeface Modern Stamp is pretty cool. Choose that typeface by clicking on the name Modern Stamp, as shown on the next page. Click and drag on the square on the left-hand side of the column until you can see the Modern Stamp in the box. Remember from the last chapter that dragging on a box this way is called scrolling. By scrolling, you can see more type sizes. Once you click to select Modern Stamp, you will see the big letter A in the box change to this typeface. Notice how strong the letter looks? This is a good typeface for making signs because the letters have thick, clear lines and can be seen from far away. (If Modern Stamp is not visible in the box, drag the scroll bar as shown to move down the list of typefaces.)

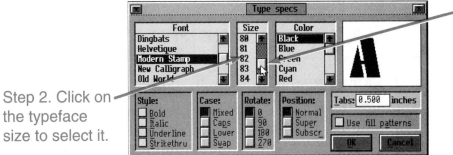

*Clicking on the name of a typeface selects it. You can
see your choice in the window at the right in the box.*

Step 9. Now it's time to make the letters in your sentence BIG
enough for a sign. In the Type Specs box you'll see a box called
SIZE. In this box you can see some numbers. These numbers tell
the computer how big to make the letters. Click and drag on the
square on the left-hand side of the column until you can see the

number 100 in the box. When you can see the number 100, stop.
Now, click once on the number 100 to choose it.

*To change the type size, drag the box as shown until the
correct size shows. Then click once on the size (100) to*

select it.

Step 10. Now, click the OK button to put the Type Specs box away. What do you see on the page? You should see giant letters that almost jump off the screen! The letters should also be in the typeface Modern Stamp. Amazing, isn't it?

Step 11. Unless you are working on a very big computer monitor, you can now see only the first few words of your sign. To see the rest of the sign, you need to tell EnVision to show you the whole page. This is done by making the page smaller on the monitor so you can see the entire page at one time. This process is called *zooming*. To see the whole page, you *zoom out*.

You can also *zoom in*. This magnifies the page. Why would you want to be able to zoom in instead of seeing the entire page at one time? By zooming in and making the page larger than it really is, you can see more details. This allows you to check your document to make sure that everything is exactly where you want it on the page.

The Zoom Tool

Zoom! Zoom! Zoom! The ZOOM button in EnVision is on the top of the Control Bar on the left hand side. It looks like a magnifying glass. There is a plus + and a minus - sign at the bottom of the magnifying glass. To see more of your sign, ZOOM OUT by clicking once on the plus sign underneath the magnifying glass. This will tell EnVision to shrink the page to half its normal size on the computer screen. After you click, you will see the whole page at one time. To make the sign look bigger again, click on the minus sign. All this zooming in and zooming out doesn't change the REAL size of the sign that will be printed—it just makes the sign look bigger or smaller on your monitor.

Click here to zoom out. This lets you see more of the page.

Click here to zoom in. This lets you magnify part of the page to see more.

Clicking on the - (minus) button of the Zoom Tool lets you see all of the sign at one time.

Step 12.   Earlier in the chapter you learned about the style called italic. When you make a word italic, it makes it the word more visible or tells people that this is a very special, important word. For fun, you can make the words Creative Kid At Work stand out from the rest of the sign so people really get the message.

   Since you don't want to make all the words in the sentence italic, you need to use a different way of selecting words, so ONLY the words Creative Kid At Work will be changed.

   To select ONLY the words Creative Kid At Work, move the cursor to the letter C. Then hold the left button down and drag the mouse over the words until they all change to WHITE letters with a black border. This selects only the words you drag over, instead of the entire sentence. Release the button on the mouse and the words will remain selected.

Step 13. Now, click once on the *I* in the Control Bar. The type will instantly become italic! (Or, you can also use the Text pull-down menu as you did earlier to do the same thing! In EnVision there are often two or more ways of doing the same thing.)

With only the words Creative Kid At Work selected, clicking on the I button in the Control Panel changes only the selected words to the italic style.

Step 14. Your sign is almost done. Before you put on the final touches, save your sign by choosing Save... from the File pull-down menu or by clicking the button in the top right corner that contains the name of your sign.

FINISHING AND PRINTING YOUR SIGN

Now it's time to add the final details to your sign and print it. Almost any sign requires a little adjustment to make the type look just right on the paper. When you look at your sign, you may notice that the words are closer to the top of the page than the bottom. This section will show you how to center the words on the page. Then you'll add the finishing touch—a frame around the words to make the sign more visible on your door or wall. The frame makes the sign look like it was created by a real creative kid, like you!

Step 15. To adjust where the words are on the page, you need to tell EnVision exactly where the words can go. To do this, click on the Pointer Tool in the Toolbar with your mouse. (Remember that the Pointer Tool is the arrow.)

Step 16. Click once on the word Creative with your mouse. Notice how a box appears in each corner of the page. Remember from Chapter 2 that the text box is the place where the words can go. If you change the size of the text box, the words will move on the page.

Step 17. Now, click on the black square in the upper left corner with your mouse and keep the mouse button held down. Then, drag this box toward the bottom of the page. To check whether the type is centered, click once on the words so EnVision will show you the change. If it's not centered yet, click again on the words so the black squares appear and move them again. The top of the page should be the same distance to the word Creative that the bottom of the page is to the word Knock.

Move the square with your mouse button held down. Click once more with your mouse to see the words in their new place on the page.

By clicking on the words, four black rectangles appear at the corners. Drag the one in the upper left corner to center the words on the page as shown.

Step 18. Now it's time to add a frame around the sign. To draw the frame, click once on the Box Tool in the Toolbar. Then click as shown to draw the box that will become the frame.

With the Box Tool selected, click here to start drawing the frame.

Drag the mouse to here to finish the frame.

By clicking on the words, four black rectangles appear at the corners. Drag the one in the upper left corner to center the words on the page as shown.

Step 19. Congratulations! You have just finished your first sign. With your mouse, save your sign by choosing Save... from the File pull-down menu.

Step 20. A sign isn't much good if you can't put it up on your wall or on a door. You need to print your sign! To print it, click on the Printer button in the Control Bar and click OK in the Printer information box like you did in Chapter 2.

MOUNTING YOUR SIGN WITH GLUE

Once you have printed your sign, you may want to glue it to cardboard or stiff paper. By gluing the sign to stronger paper or cardboard, it will last longer and look better. The paper or cardboard used to make the sign stronger is called *backing material*. Backing is used to make paper stronger because you can't print on cardboard with a computer printer. The cardboard would jam the printer!

Here are things from around the house you can use as backing material for your signs:

- *Stiff paper from the cover of a magazine.*
- *A side panel from a brown cardboard box.*
- *Construction paper (Use a light color so you can't see the construction paper through the sign.)*
- *A manila folder.*
- *The cardboard from the back of a writing pad.*
- *The cover of an old phone book that's no longer in use.*

The easiest way to glue a sign to backing material is to place a small dot of glue or rubber cement on the backing, as shown. Use only a small amount to prevent the wet glue from wrinkling your sign. After putting the glue on the backing material, carefully place the sign on top and gently rub down the glued areas. Let the glue dry before you hang your sign on the wall.

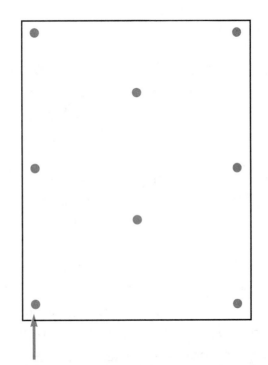

Apply a small dot of glue or rubber cement as shown to the back of your sign to mount it to a piece of cardboard or stiff paper. Don't use too much glue or the sign may become wrinkled.

If the backing material is larger than the sign, after the glue is fully dry, use scissors to trim off the extra paper or cardboard.

CREATE-IT ON YOUR OWN

When you create signs, you will always use steps like the ones you just completed. Here is a summary of the steps you can follow to make more signs.

Step 1. Start EnVision.

Step 2. Type in the words you want to put on the sign. (Make sure the Text Tool is selected on the Toolbar or Control Panel.) Save your sign with a new name by using the Save As... command found under the File pull-down menu.

Step 3. Center the type if you want or move it to the right or left. (Select the type by double clicking on it with your mouse. Choose Center, Right, or Left from the Text pull-down menu.)

Step 4. Change the words to look the way you want them to look. You can change the typeface, size, and style of the words. Select the words you want to change, and then make the changes in the Type Specs box, which you can make appear by clicking with your mouse on the A in the Control Panel or by clicking on the Type Specs... command in the Text pull-down menu.

Step 5. Move the type around on the page if you want to. Click once on the words with the Pointer Tool selected. Then drag on the black squares to reshape the text box or on the black square in the center of the box to move it around the page. Click once more to see the changes.

Step 6. Add a frame. Select the Box Tool and draw a box around the type by dragging with your mouse. Reshape the box by dragging on the two empty squares on the corner. Click once more and then drag on the four black squares to reshape the box. Or, use the black square in the center of the box to move it around the page. Click once more to see your changes.

Step 7. Save your sign by choosing Save from the File pull-down menu.

Step 8. Print your sign by choosing Print from the File pull-down menu or clicking on the Printer button in the Control Panel. Click OK in the Printer control box to print your sign.

Step 9. Quit EnVision by choosing Exit from the File pull-down menu.

MORE SIGN IDEAS

Now the you know the basics of creating signs, you can use the same steps to create signs with all kinds of messages. Here are some ideas for signs you can make.

☞ *Make a sign with your name on it for inside your locker at school.*

☞   Put a name sign on your
bedroom door at home.

☞   Make name signs
for your parents to
use at work.

☞   Make a sign with
the name of your favorite
sports team on it and hang
it on your wall at home or
school.

☞   Make signs with
happy   or   fun
messages like
"Make My Day," or "Be Cool," or "Don't Have a
Cow, Man!" Hang them in your room or give
them to friends.

☞   Make signs to tell people where you are.
For example, the signs could say, "I'm at school
now," or "I'm at baseball practice," or "I'm at
dancing lessons." Put a sign on your door so
your friends and family can find you.

Of course, making signs with only words on them
might get boring after a while. You probably want to know
how to add pictures and symbols to your signs. In the next
chapter, you're going to learn how to do just that!

4. START YOUR OWN BUSINESS— CREATE AN ADVERTISING FLYER!

Is your allowance money leaving you a little short on cash? If so, you can make extra money by starting your own business. It's easy to do, although it takes a little thinking to decide on a business that's right for you. You should choose work that you have both the skills and the equipment to carry out. After working through *The Create-It Kit*, if you have your own computer and printer, you can start a desktop publishing business. (More on that at the end of this chapter.) But there are lots of other businesses that you can start that don't require anything but a little work on your part. Here are a few ideas:

- Lawnmowing service
- Dog walking service
- Houseminding service for vacationing neighbors
- Sweeping service for local businesses
- Sweeping services for apartment complexes
- Grocery pick-up service
- Snow shoveling and leaf raking service
- Car washing and waxing service
- Recycling service
- Window washer
- Party photographer

How about a business walking the neighbor's dog?

For more kid's business ideas and how to make them work, look up *Better than a Lemonade Stand: Small Business Ideas for Kids*, a book by Daryl Bernstein (ISBN number 0-941831-75-2, $7.95 at your local book store). Written by fifteen-year-old Daryl, it's got lots of great ideas for fun businesses and tells you how to set up and run them. Daryl started his first business when he was only eight years old.

IT PAYS TO ADVERTISE!

The hardest part of starting a business is getting customers. You need to let people know about your business and what you can do for them. While you can knock on doors in your neighborhood, advertising is a much better way to let people know that you're available. If you create one ad, hundreds of people may see it. Even if only a few people see the ad and call you, you may get more work than you can handle!

**Maybe a
lawnmowing
business
would be fun?**

It's expensive to print an ad in a newspaper or magazine, but there's an inexpensive kind of advertising done with flyers. Flyers are ads printed on paper that fits in your computer's printer. This chapter will show you how to make a flyer for your business. Once you've created a flyer, you can print a bunch of copies and deliver them to potential customers. You can walk around your neighborhood and place your flyers on people's doors or drop them off to local businesses. The flyer should have your phone number on it so people can call to buy your services. It's that easy. Then, sit back and wait for the phone to ring with jobs. But, first, you need to make the flyer!

After reading this chapter, you will know how to make a flyer for almost any kind of business. A template is included with the book for making flyers. Clip art is included for many businesses that kids can start.

WAIT A MINUTE! WHAT ARE TEMPLATES AND CLIP ART?

When EnVision Publisher was installed on your computer, a bunch of things called *templates* and *clip art* were installed with it. These were made just for *The Create-It Kit*. But what are they?

Remember how you saved your sign by using the Save... command and giving the sign a name? A template is a special publication that's kept on the hard disk.

Consider starting a leaf raking company in the fall.

If you opened your sign file again, you could make a new sign just by typing in new words because the hard part is already done. You don't have to move the text box again or add another border. It's already been done to the sign and the computer remembers that. But, if you want to keep the original sign, you couldn't type over it and save it

This is the template you will use to make your flyer. All you have to do is type a few words and bring in a picture. You can use this template over and over again for any kind of business!

again. Only the new sign would be saved and the old one would be gone.

Templates are used so you make publications that look the same but with new words and pictures. A template is very similar to a saved document like your sign, but when you save your new publication it doesn't change the template. The template remains the same so you can use it over and over again. The templates are saved on your computer's hard disk. In this chapter, you will use a template for making a flyer. The template has the text boxes already set up. With a template you can create a flyer much faster than if you had to start from scratch.

Templates have slightly different names than publications. Remember how you saved your sign in the last chapter? It was saved as SIGN1.EVP. The .EVP is short for EnVision Publisher. Templates are saved differently so that EnVision Publisher won't let you accidentally lose one by giving a publication the same name. Templates in EnVision are saved with a .EVT on the end. The T at the end is for template. If you had saved your sign as a template, it would have been saved with as SIGN1.EVT instead of SIGN1.EVP.

The Create-It Kit comes with lots of clip art pictures! There is a catalog of them at the back of the book.

OKAY, OKAY! BUT WHAT'S CLIP ART?

Clip art is a collection of pictures that you can add to your publications. *The Create-It Kit* comes with a bunch of cool pictures that were drawn by John Wincek. You can use them to make your publications look fantastic. In this chapter, you'll learn how to add these pictures to the flyer you create. Pictures are included for all sorts of holidays and special occasions.

IMPRESS YOUR FRIENDS!

The first flyer you're going to make is for a lawnmowing business. But, you can change it to make it work for almost any kind of company. At the end of the chapter you'll learn how to change it. Put the lawnmowing flyer together first, so you'll know how to make one. Then you can make your own to promote a business or to announce a special event in your school or neighborhood. Start EnVision Publisher first. Then follow the steps for making the flyer.

 ### HOW TO OPEN A TEMPLATE

Step 1. From the File pull-down menu, choose the command Open... An information box will appear. Click on the Template button. That tells EnVision to show you a list of templates you can use.

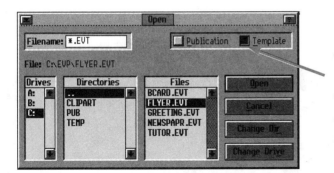

To open a template, click here to tell EnVision to show you a list of templates. If you click on Publication, it will show you a list of publications on the disk.

Step 2. Click on the FLYER.EVT name in the list under Files. This selects the template. Click the Open button to open it.

Step 3. The flyer template will appear on your screen. Now that the template is open, you need to zoom out like you did in the last chapter. Click on the minus sign on the Zoom button in the Control Bar to zoom out. This will let you see the whole page on your monitor at one time.

Now that the template is open, you can see that it looks much different than the plain blank page. There are already text boxes and borders in place. That is how a template saves you time. Instead of having to draw each box and format its type, you select the words already there and type your own words to replace them. The same template can be used to make many different flyers. If a lawnmowing business slows down in the fall, you can

Everyone wants their walks shoveled after a snowstorm. This might be a good business opportunity.

quickly use the template to make a flyer for a leaf raking business. And, you can make a snow shoveling flyer in the winter from the same template. You just change the words and picture, which we'll show you how to do now.

CREATE A HEADLINE FOR YOUR FLYER

A headline is the most important part of your flyer. The headline is usually the first sentence you see when you look at an advertisement or flyer, so you want it to say something important to get people's attention.

Do this: Find a copy of a magazine or newspaper around the house and flip through it. Notice how almost every ad has one sentence in big type? This is the headline.

It is used to tell the reader what is for sale and to convince people to buy a product.

Your flyer needs a headline too. The template has a text box that says Headline inside. Here is where you will tell people what you are selling. This will get people who see your flyer to call you and order your services.

DO IT

HOW TO MAKE THE HEADLINE FOR A FLYER

Step 1. Using the Text Tool, click once on the text box with the word Headline to make it active. Then, double click on the word Headline in the flyer template. This will select it. Type:

I will mow your lawn for $5.00 a week!

This is your headline. As you type the headline, EnVision makes the text the right size and makes it bold too. This was

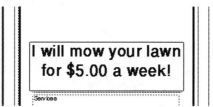

set up in the template to make it easier to put your flyer together. Of course, you can decide how much to charge your customers. The best way to decide on a price is to find out what other kids in the neighborhood charge. You should charge the same amount per week or a little less if you want to get more business. An adult can help you decide on prices for your services.

WHAT SERVICES WILL YOU SELL?

Of course you should tell people more about your lawnmowing business than will fit in the headline. Because this information isn't as important as your headline, the words for this section are set in smaller type. That way, your readers see the headline first. The smaller type also has a name in the advertising business. It's called *body copy*. It's what people read after reading the headline.

You can explain your extra services and prices in the body copy. You can also explain more about your business. Here are some examples of body copy for a flyer:

I will mow your lawn once a week and pick up the grass clippings.

I can also provide these services:

> Leaf Raking—$2.00 a week
> Bush Trimming—$2.00 a week
> Lawn Edging—$2.00 a week

Write the body copy on a piece of paper along with prices before you type it in. (Keep in mind that in advertising the word copy simply means words and sentences.) Don't write too many words. Fewer words are better in a flyer because most readers don't want to read an advertisement that's too long. The text box in the template will hold about 60 words, but 25 to 35 words is usually enough.

Now, it's time to add the rest of the copy to your flyer. Here are the steps to follow.

HOW TO ADD THE BODY COPY

DO IT *Step 1.* Use the Zoom Tool to see your flyer better (click the minus sign once). Then, drag on the Elevator Bar on the right of the screen to scroll to the middle of the flyer. This will let you see the text box where you can add more information to your flyer.

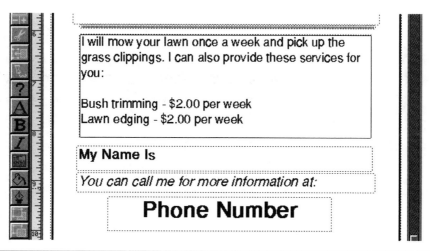

Step 2. With the Text Tool selected, click once on the text box containing the word Services to select it. Then double click on the word Services to select the word.

Step 3. Type the body copy you wrote on paper into this box. When you start typing, you'll see the word Services is replaced with your typing. If the copy won't fit, do what's called *cutting the copy*. Erase some words from your copy to make it shorter. If you type more words then will fit, EnVision will add small + signs at the bottom of the box. The + means that some words have been pushed out of the box because there's not enough room.

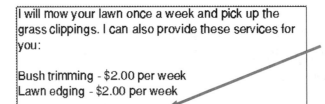

These plus signs mean that there are too many words to fit in the text box.

Step 4. You want your customers to know your name and how to reach you. Otherwise, how will they know who to call? The flyer has a space for you to type your name and to enter your phone number. Enter your name by clicking once on the text box containing the words My Name Is. Click with the Text Tool once after the words and then type your name. You can use just your first name or both your first name and last name.

Changing Words and Fixing Mistakes

Sometimes you may make a mistake or type more words than will fit in a text box. Here is how to fix mistakes:

Step 1. To change a letter or word, or delete it, click on it once the text box with the Text Tool to make it active.

Step 2. Click once in front of the word to insert the pointer.

Step 3. Drag over the word or words with the left mouse button held down. This will select them.

Step 4. Press the Delete Key to erase the word. Or, type the new word or correction. The new typing will replace the selected word instantly.

To erase or change a paragraph:

Step 1. Click on it once on the text box with the Text Tool to make the text box active.

Step 2. Double click anywhere in the paragraph to select it. Press the Delete Key to erase the paragraph. Or, type your changes and the new words will replace the old paragraph.

Step 5. Type your phone number in the box at the bottom. Remember to click once to make the box active with the Text Tool. Then double click on the words Phone Number and type your phone number. Check with an adult for permission to use the phone number in the flyer.

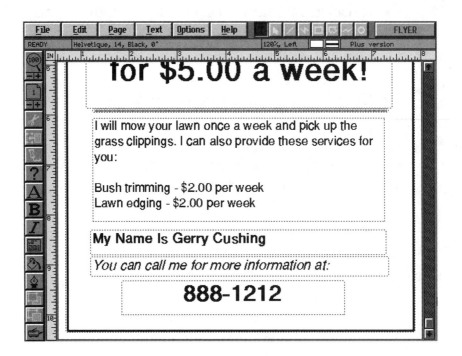

That's it. You now have a flyer complete with all of the words! But wait, there's one more step. You need to paste a picture onto your flyer. A picture will help the flyer get noticed. *The Create-It Kit* comes with a clip art picture for a lawnmowing business. Follow these steps to bring in the picture into your flyer.

Step 1. Click anywhere on the page except on a text box or the border. This ensures that none of the text boxes at the bottom of the page are still active. (If a text box is active, instead of importing a picture, EnVision will assume you want to import words.)

Step 2. Click on the File button to display the pull-down menu. Choose the Import... command. An information box will appear.

Step 3. A list of pictures will appear under the word Files. Use the miniature Elevator Bar next to this list and drag its box a little at a time, until you can see the name MOWER.PCX. Click once on this name to select it. Then click the Import button in the box. This will make the box

You can find more pictures for your business flyers in the clip art catalog at the back of the book. For example, this picture could be used for a business that makes videotapes of special events.

disappear from your screen.

Step 4. EnVision automatically zooms out to let you place your picture. A small camera will appear on your screen. That means EnVision is ready to paste a picture into your flyer. Position the camera at the top of the flyer. The camera is a pointer that shows where EnVision will paste your picture. Click once to paste the picture. Wait about five seconds for your picture to appear before doing anything else.

Step 5. The picture was probably pasted into your flyer in the wrong place. It's probably too small as well. Here's how to fix it. With the Pointer Tool selected, click once on the picture to make it active. You'll see little black squares appear. Make the picture bigger by dragging any of the black squares at the corner of the picture.

Step 6.   Click on the square at the center of the picture and drag on it to move the picture to the top and center of your flyer. Make sure it is centered on the page before letting go of the mouse button. Then, once it's placed where you want it, click once on a blank part of the page. This will tell EnVision that the picture is placed where you want it.

Step 7. Save the flyer as FLYER.EVP by using the Save As... command from the File Menu as you've done before.

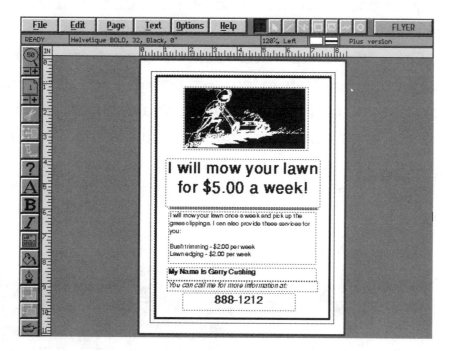

This is how your flyer should look on your monitor once it's complete. If the picture is still a little off center, click on it once with the Pointer Tool and drag the black square at the center to adjust its position.

IT'S TIME TO PRINT YOUR FLYER!

That's it—you're ready to go into business!. To print your flyer, follow the printing directions from the last chapter. Print one flyer and check the spelling of all of the words. This is called *proofreading.* You should proofread your publications to make sure that everything is spelled correctly and that there are no other mistakes. Make sure that your phone number is correct! If it isn't, your customers won't be able to reach you.

Once you're sure everything is correct, you'll want to print a bunch of flyers to leave at people's houses. There are two ways you can print your flyer. You can print a bunch of copies on your computer's printer. You can also take make copies on a copy machine. Ask an adult which way is best because some computer printers use expensive ink and paper.

Print one copy of your flyer to check the spelling. Then, enter the number of copies you want in the Print information box. Print enough to hand out or make copies on a copy machine.

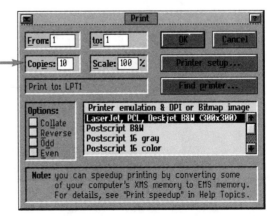

To print more than one copy at a time, tell EnVision how many copies you want to print in the Print information box. Type in the number of copies in the Copies box, as shown. EnVision can print from 1 to 99 copies.

You can print your flyer on colored paper if your computer's printer let's you print on single sheets of paper. Colored paper can also be used in most copy machines. You can buy colored copy paper from an office supply store. Most stores that do copying sell colored paper too.

Once you print the flyer for your business, walk around your neighborhood and leave it at the door of houses with

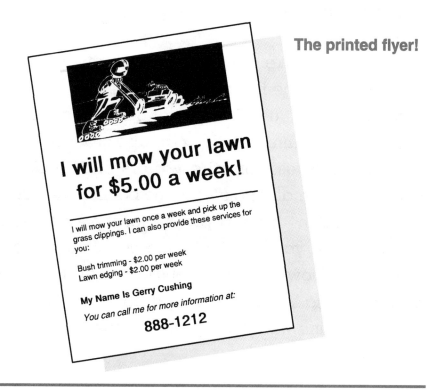

The printed flyer!

lawns. The ones where the grass is long may be the best customers for your business. After you hand out your flyers, try to stay near the telephone in case a customer calls. If you can't be around the phone because of school, an answering machine can help. When people call, answer their questions courteously and try to set up a regular day for cutting their lawn. As you take on jobs, have an adult work with you to collect payments and make sure that your business runs smoothly.

MAKING FLYERS FOR OTHER BUSINESSES

You can make a flyer for almost any kind of business. The catalog at the back of the book shows the name of the pictures you can use. You paste them into your flyers using the Import... command. You can also order a second disk of clip art pictures from the writers of *The Create-It Kit*. Ordering information is also at the back of the book.

If you don't have a picture for the kind business you want to start, you can make the headline bigger to fill up the page. Follow the instructions for making the type bigger and changing the size of the text box from the last chapter. A big headline will catch your customer's attention just like a picture does.

HOW ABOUT STARTING A DESKTOP PUBLISHING BUSINESS?

If you have your own computer and printer, you can start a desktop publishing business. You can make flyers for other kids to use or to announce special events for school.

To get started, you can make a flyer to promote your new company. Use the picture of the desktop publishing mouse that came with the book. The picture is called DTPMOUSE.PCX.

Use this mouse as the picture in a flyer for your new desktop publishing business!

Once you work through *The Create-It Kit*, you will know how to make all kinds of publications for your customers, like greeting cards, invitations, and even newspapers!

WHAT ELSE CAN YOU USE FLYERS FOR?

You can make flyers for purposes other than advertising a business. Here are just a few ideas to get you started:

- Create a flyer to promote a school play or a concert.
- Make a flyer to announce a party.
- Use flyers to tell people about sports events.

Now you know how to make flyers, use templates, and import pictures, You're really getting the hang of this desktop publishing stuff. In the next chapter, you'll learn how to make greeting cards for your friends and family. There's still a lot more publishing fun ahead!

5. MAKE SOMETHING SPECIAL— CREATE YOUR OWN GREETING CARDS!

Everyone likes getting a birthday card on their special day. But, instead of going to the store and buying people ordinary birthday cards, why not make them yourself? A card that you make will mean more to

Byte loves to read the funny cards at the drugstore. They always make him laugh.

Bit likes to get funny greeting cards too!

your friends and family than one purchased at a store. Anyone can buy a birthday card, but not everyone can make one.

You can make your own birthday cards with EnVision Publisher. This chapter will show you how! And, once you know how to make birthday cards, you can make greeting cards for every holiday including Christmas, Mother's Day, Hanukkah, and even Groundhog Day! *The Create-It Kit* comes with clip art pictures for many holidays and special occasions that you can use in your cards.

WHO THOUGHT UP THE IDEA OF GREETING CARDS ANYWAY?

No one knows who came up with the idea of greeting

cards. It is known that the ancient Egyptians traded New Year's cards way back in the 6th century BC. It seems those Egyptians were first with everything when it came to writing!

Before it became Valentine's Day, this holiday was celebrated by exchanging greeting cards in ancient Rome. The holiday became a day for people to give friendship cards to their family and friends. Today, this holiday is more than 2,000 years old and cards are still exchanged.

Desktop publishing lets you make greeting cards for all kinds of occasions. You can print cards for everyone in your family and for all your friends. It's easy to make cards with *The Create-It Kit* because you put your cards together using templates and clip art, just like you made the flyer in the last chapter.

Here are some of the clip art pictures that you can use for making greeting cards!

TURN YOUR PAPER ON ITS SIDE!

Your first greeting card will be printed a new way, called *landscape mode*. To see what this means, find a greeting card around the house. It doesn't matter what holiday the card was for. Open it up and place it next to the flyer you printed in the last chapter. What is different about the printing on the flyer and the open card?

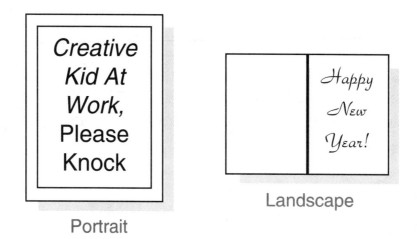

Portrait

Landscape

The card's paper is wider than it's tall. But, the flyer is taller than it's wide. (A few cards are printed taller than they are wide, but these are less common.)

Your flyer is printed in *portrait mode*. Think of a portrait of George Washington or Abe Lincoln. Portraits are taller than they are wide. When greeting cards are opened, they are usually wider than they are tall, just like a painting of a

Portrait   Portrait

Landscape

landscape is usually wider than it is tall. When the card is folded in half, it will be taller than it is wide. Folding gives the card a front cover and an inside where you can put another message and sign your name.

A GREETING CARD IS PRINTED ON TWO SIDES OF THE PAPER

If you still have your store-bought greeting card handy, look how it's printed on both sides of the paper. The birthday card you'll make in this chapter will be printed the same way. But, instead of having two different EnVision publications—one for each side of the card—you'll learn how to make a single EnVision publication with two pages! That's right. You can create publications containing more than one page. In fact, EnVision lets you have up 120 pages in a single publication. That's enough to write a book! But for now, you'll just learn how to make a two-page greeting card. You can make bigger documents later.

A greeting card template was installed on your computer's hard disk with EnVision Publisher. It's called GREETING.EVT and it was created in landscape mode. Now let's open the template and make a birthday card!

DO IT

HOW TO CREATE THE FRONT OF A BIRTHDAY CARD!

Step 1. Open the template called GREETING.EVT the same way you opened the flyer template in the last chapter. (In case you're wondering about the line in the middle of the card, it's to show you where to fold the card in half when it's done.)

In Case You Forgot...

To open the template, choose the command Open... from the File pull-down menu. An information box will open on your monitor. In that box, click on the Template button. That tells EnVision to show you a list of templates you can use instead of EnVision publications such as your sign. Click on the name GREETING.EVT in the list under Files. This selects the template. Click the Open button to open the template. The greeting card template will then appear on your screen.

Step 2. Save the birthday card as BIRTHDAY.EVP.

Step 3. Now that the template is open, you need to zoom out like you've done before. This will let you see the entire card instead of just the corner. Click on the minus sign on the Zoom button to zoom out.

The template called GREETING.EVT is made up of two pages, not just one like the flyer template. You can jump from page to page by clicking on the Page button on the Control Bar. This button moves you from page to page in a publication with more than one page. It works something like the Zoom button. You click on the plus sign to go to the next page or the minus sign to go back a page. You can always tell what page you're on by looking at the button. A number on the button tells you the number of the page on your screen.

Click on the - to go to the previous page.➡ ⬅ Click on the + to go to the next page.

Step 4. Click the plus sign on the Page button to jump to page 2. See how the second page looks different than the first. That's because page 2 will become the inside of the card and page 1 will be the outside.

Step 5. Since you will assemble the card's front cover first, click on the minus sign in the Page button to go back to page 1. It should look like this on your computer's monitor.

Step 6. To make a great birthday card, you need to type a great message on the front of the card. With the Text Tool selected, click once on the word Greeting on the card's front cover. Then double click on the word to select it.

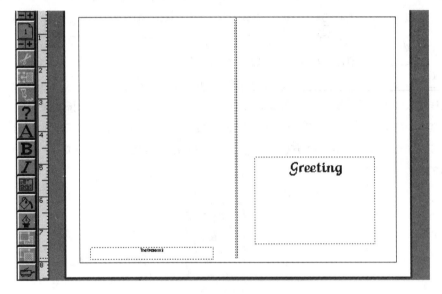

Step 7. Type the greeting shown in the box. Use exclamation marks (!) to make it more exciting!

Cool!
It's your birthday!

After entering the word Cool!, press the Enter key to put the these words on the next line.

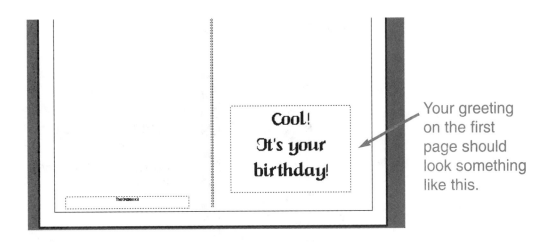

Your greeting on the first page should look something like this.

Step 8. Add a birthday party picture to the card. Here's a birthday party picture from the clip art catalog that's perfect. Use the Import... command like your did in the last chapter. The birthday picture is called BIRTHDAY.PCX. If you've used the Import... command correctly, you will see the pointer turn into a little camera.

Click on the card's cover to paste the picture on the page.

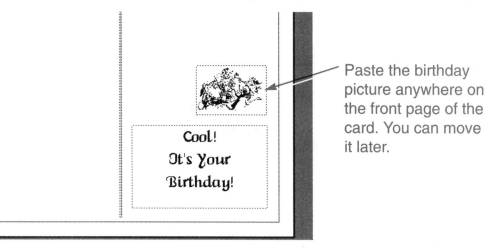

Paste the birthday picture anywhere on the front page of the card. You can move it later.

Step 9. Center the picture on the card by using the Pointer Tool. The card should look something like this.

WANT A BIGGER PICTURE?

You can make the birthday party picture bigger if you want to. To change it, click once on it with the Pointer Tool. You'll see the five black squares appear. Click on a black square in any corner and drag to make the box bigger.

Then to see the new size, click anywhere once with the Pointer Tool selected. Here's what the front of the card looks like with a bigger picture.

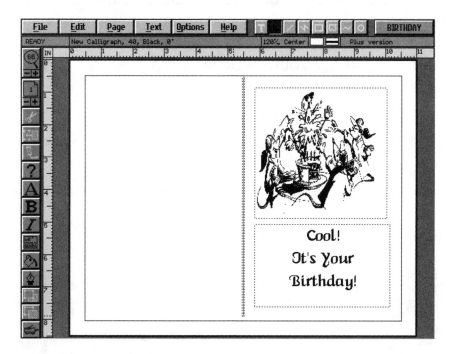

That's it, you've created the cover for a birthday card. Now it's time to put a message on the inside of the card.

DO IT HOW TO CREATE PAGE 2 OF THE CARD

Step 1. Click the Page button on the plus sign, to go to page 2, which is the inside of the card. (Remember to click on an empty space on the page before going to page 2. Nothing will happen if a box is still selected.) If you do it correctly, you will see a text box with the word Greeting.

Step 2. Click once on the text box after selecting the Text Tool to make it active. Then double click on the word Greeting to select it.

Step 3. Make up your own birthday greeting. If you can't think of one, type in this one:

Hope it's a smashing day!!

Here's what is will look like on the inside of the card.

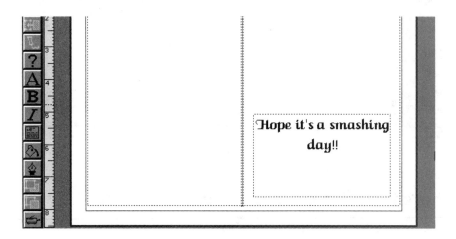

That should do it. Of course, there are other birthday pictures you can use on your card. You can even put a picture on the inside if you want to. Just pick one of the pictures from the catalog at the back of the book and put it inside with your message. You already know the steps.

PRINTING THE CARD

Now it's time to print your card. You will need to print on two sides of a single sheet of paper and that takes a little bit of practice. You have to experiment to learn how to put the paper through the printer. If you do it wrong, you might print the inside of the card upside down. You might print one side on top of the other side. You might even make both mistakes! Don't worry. Just practice until you get it right.

You may wonder how you can print on both sides of the same piece of paper. It's easy for most computer printers. You simply print one side of a single sheet of paper. Then you turn it over and put it back through your printer to print the other side. The way you flip and turn the paper will depend on the kind of printer you use.

With dot-matrix and ink-jet printers, you print the first side of the paper by manually feeding it to the printer, just like you would put paper into a typewriter. On laser printers, you will use the Manual Feed to run the paper through the printer one side at a time. It's much easier than it sounds, but if you can't figure it out, don't wait to ask someone for help. Here are the basic steps to follow for printing your greeting card.

HOW TO PRINT BOTH SIDES OF THE CARD

Step 1. Click on the Print button in the Control Bar. The Print information box will open. In the From: and To: boxes, enter 1. This will print only the cover of the card (page 1). Click the OK button to print the cover of the card.

To print the card's cover, enter a 1 in the From: and To: boxes. This tells EnVision to only print the first page.

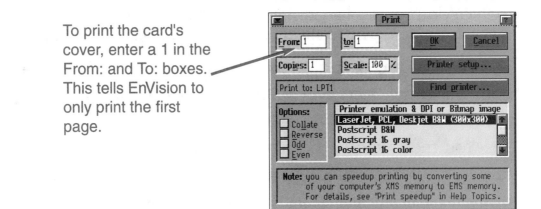

Step 2. Remove the printed card cover from your printer. Flip it as shown on the next page and load it back into your printer. Now you can print the inside of the card.

Before Turning the Paper   After Turning the Paper

WHAT IF YOUR PRINTER USES PAPER THAT YOU HAVE TO TEAR?

If your printer uses paper that you have to tear, tear the card off carefully. Remove the rest of the paper from the printer. Turn the page over and insert the card the same way you would put a sheet of paper into a typewriter.

Step 3. With the paper loaded into the printer, click on the Print button. In the Print information box, tell EnVision which page you want to print. Do this by typing 2 into the From: box and 2 in the To: box. This tells EnVision to print only page 2 which is the inside of your card. Click the OK button to print the inside of your card.

WHAT IF IT COMES OUT WRONG?

If your card prints wrong, follow the printing steps again, but change the way you print the inside. Here's what to do:

☞ If the cover and inside print on top of each other: print the cover again. Then, when you insert the paper to print the inside, don't flip it this time. This should fix the problem.

☞ If the inside of your card prints upside down: print the cover again. Then, when you insert the paper to print the inside, flip it backward, then turn the paper around. This should fix the problem.

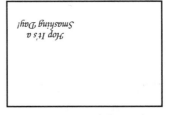

Before Flipping Paper   After Flipping Paper

FINISHING YOUR CARD

Give three cheers! You've made your first birthday card! To finish the card, fold it carefully along the line in the middle of the cover. To make the fold look better, gently rub the bowl of a spoon along the edge of the fold. This will make it look smoother.

You should sign the inside of the card with your name and write a short message, too. In a birthday card, you might write a message like this before you sign your name:

I hope you have the happiest
of birthdays!

You can give your finished card directly to the person you made it for. Or, if you are giving the person a gift, tape the card to the outside or put it inside the gift box. Since you made the card yourself, instead of just buying it at the store, it will probably make the person who gets it especially happy.

YOU CAN MAKE CARDS FOR MANY OCCASIONS

Now that you know how to make a birthday card, you can make greeting cards or invitations for almost any special occasion. Just choose from the clip art pictures that starts on page 185. Create your own messages and greetings and enter them in the template. Follow the steps for printing your cards and you're done! You can make a card for every occasion. Here are few ideas for other cards you can create with the clip art pictures.

Christmas cards and other holiday cards.

Merry Christmas!

Watch the Big Game with Us

Invitations to watch a sporting event or go to a game.

You can create Valentine's Day cards for all your friends and family.

You're Invited to a Party!

Happy Valentine's Day!

Party invitations for special holidays, like Halloween.

Thank You Thank You Thank you!

There are even more ideas in the catalog. Go for it. Make cards for any reason at all. It doesn't have to be a special day. Create a card to tell your Mom that you love her. Make a card to tell your best friend that you really liked the party you went to last week. Now that you can make your own cards, you can make a card whenever you think of something nice that you want to say to someone. It's a great way to make other people happy and you'll feel good about it too!

Now that you're an experienced desktop publisher

who can print two-page documents, it's time to try a bigger project. In the next chapter, you will become a reporter and make your own neighborhood newspaper!

6. BE AN ACE REPORTER— PUBLISH YOUR OWN NEWSPAPER!

There are more newspapers published in the world than any other kind of publication. According to *Grolier's Academic American Encyclopedia*, about 60,000 newspapers are published in the world, and these papers are bought by more than 500,000,000 people. Since most papers are read by more than one person, the actual number of people who regularly read newspapers may be more than 1,500,000,000.

(That's one and a half BILLION people.) Wow! That's almost half the people in the world!

People read newspapers because there are always things they need to know about. People depend on newspapers to find out what's happening. Because of this, reporters who write about the news and the publishers who print the newspapers are very important people.

If you like to go places and observe what's happening, you can be an ace reporter who gathers hot scoops on news and events from around the school and neighborhood. You should take a notebook with you to write about the news. When you ask people questions about an event, you should write down their names and their answers to the questions. This is important because you want to be accurate when you write the news.

After gathering your news stories, you can go back to your computer and use your notes to write stories for your newspaper. You can use EnVision Publisher to put the newspaper together. After the paper is printed, you can deliver copies to your family, friends, classmates, or neighbors. You might even want to sell subscriptions to the paper to make some money. You'll also be a respected person in the neighborhood, because you will help people keep up with the news.

BE THE PUBLISHER IN YOUR NEIGHBORHOOD

Being a reporter sounds exciting, doesn't it? There is a special template for a newspaper on your hard disk that was installed with EnVision Publisher. The template makes it easy for you to create a newspaper on your computer. With your new desktop publishing skills, you can also become the publisher of the newspaper—one of the most important people on the newspaper staff. The publisher runs the paper and coordinates things to make sure the paper gets printed and delivered on time.

There is news in every neighborhood and school. Together, you, your friends, family members, and classmates can write stories for the newspaper. You can also add clip art and pictures to the paper to make the newspaper more interesting. This chapter will show you how to add pictures from other programs so you can use your own art as well as the clip art that comes with *The Create-It Kit.*

If you want to create a newspaper every week or every month, maybe you can get some of your classmates involved and make it a school project. Some people could be reporters. Others could be editors. Editors are the people

who make sure the stories are written correctly. They also decide where the news should go in the paper. People could take turns being the publisher, who coordinates everything.

If you want to publish a paper every week or every month, you should develop a publishing schedule. The schedule should say when the news stories need to be done, when the stories are entered into the EnVision Publisher template, and when the paper should be distributed.

If you don't want to publish a newspaper very often, you can publish one when there's something special going on, like a softball championship, school play, or visit with an important relative. This kind of paper would be called a "special issue."

THE THREE STEPS IN NEWSPAPER PRODUCTION

There are three steps to putting a newspaper together. The first step is to get the news. The second step is to assemble all the information and put it into the format of a newspaper. This is where your desktop publishing skills will be used. The third step is to print the newspaper. After the paper is printed, it must be delivered to the people who want to read the news.

STEP ONE—GETTING THE NEWS

You need to gather enough news to fill up your newspaper. You can write stories on lots of subjects. When you gather and write news, you are a *reporter*. The choice of news topics is up to you. If you see something interesting happening, just ask the people who are involved to tell you about it. If you write a story about the event, you are *reporting* the news. You can write about almost anything in your newspaper, but the stories should be of interest to the people who will read your paper.

If you are doing a newspaper for your family, stories about family activities such as vacations and the news about changes around the house are of interest to your readers. For a newspaper that will be distributed to

This friend of Byte's is a reporter for *The Mouse News*.

classmates, stories on school activities and after-school events will be most interesting. You might even add features on the weather and the latest trends in fashions if there's room for them. Crossword puzzles and games in a newspaper are interesting to almost everyone, so include them if you can.

If you have too many stories, you can always save some of the less important ones for another edition of your paper. If you're short on news, watch the news on TV or read the daily paper from your city for more ideas.

STEP TWO—PUTTING IT ALL TOGETHER

Once the news is collected, you need to assemble your paper. In newspaper lingo, this is called *composing*, and when you compose a newspaper, you become a *compositor!* As a desktop publisher you will use EnVision Publisher and the template that came with the book to compose your newspaper.

STEP THREE—ROLL THE PRESSES!

Once you have composed the paper, it's time to roll the presses to get your newspaper out on time. You can print the copies on your computer's printer. If you plan to distribute the paper to a lot of people, it might be faster and cheaper to make photocopies of the paper. You will learn how to do this later in the chapter.

The Presses

THE PARTS OF THE NEWSPAPER

The first newspapers were produced by the ancient

Romans, but newspapers became popular in Europe after 1650 A.D., when printing technology made it fast and affordable to produce regular newspapers. Over the years, newspapers have adopted a standard format using columns and five basic parts.

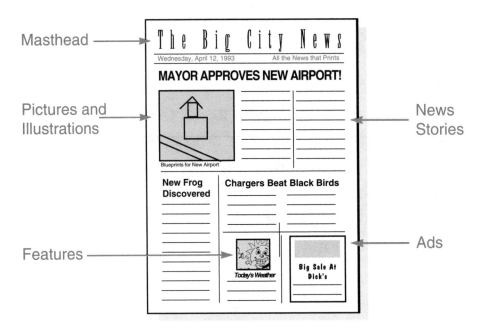

Masthead

Pictures and Illustrations

News Stories

Features

Ads

The Parts of a Newspaper

The five parts included in almost every newspaper are:

1. The *masthead*. The masthead includes the title of the paper, the name and location of the publisher, and the date of publication.

2. The *news stories*. Most newspapers have more than one story. Each story also has a headline.

3. *Pictures or illustrations*. Pictures are used to make the news more interesting and easier to understand.

4. *Features*. The features are included in each issue of a newspaper. They include things like the weather column, the comics, the television listings, or a crossword puzzle.

5. *Ads*. The ads (short for advertisements) are used to sell things or announce special events.

The newspaper template you will use with EnVision Publisher includes these five parts, as do big daily newspapers like *The New York Times* and *USA Today*.

PUTTING YOUR PAPER TOGETHER

The number of stories and features in your paper will determine how big your paper is going to be. For your family, just filling in the front page might be enough. For a school project that you do by yourself, a two- or three- page paper might be good. But, if your paper is a class project, then four pages or even more might be needed to include all the stories and ideas created by your classmates.

The template for creating your own newspaper is for a

four-page newspaper, but you can create a paper of one or two pages in length if you don't have enough stories for four pages. You can also add pages to make a longer newspaper, You'll learn how to do this later in the chapter.

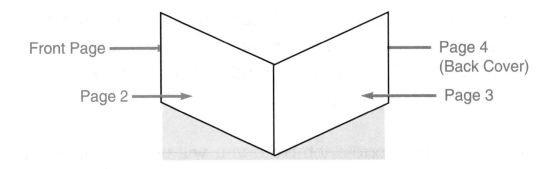

Front Page ──────→ | Page 4 (Back Cover)

Page 2 ──────→ | ←────── Page 3

To start assembling the newspaper, you need to have most of your news stories ready to type into the template. Then you can follow the steps to complete the newspaper. Here goes!

OPEN THE TEMPLATE FIRST

Use the Open... command to choose the template for the newspaper project. It's called NEWSPAPR.EVT. Don't forget to click on the Template button in the Open information box so that you can see the list of templates.

After opening the template, you'll see that it has three columns. That is where your news stories will go.

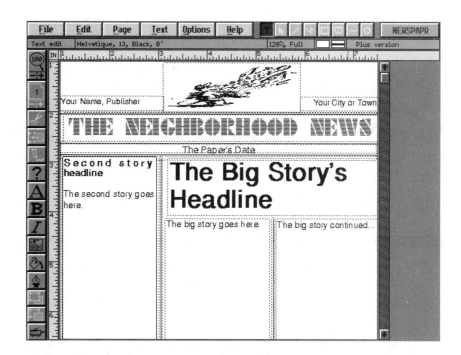

CREATE THE MASTHEAD

The first thing you'll want to do is enter the masthead information. The name of your newspaper is in the masthead. The masthead also contains the date the newspaper was printed and the name and location of the publisher.

The masthead goes on the top of the first page. Here are the steps for making the masthead for your paper.

HOW TO CREATE THE MASTHEAD

Step 1.   After opening the template, rename the file as

MYPAPER.EVP. Now, select the Text Tool. Then click and drag on the words Your Name to select them. Type in your own name. (Leave the word Publisher in the box because that's your title when you put a newspaper together.)

Step 2. Double click on the word Date. Now type in the date you plan to deliver your newspaper. If you will deliver your publication today, use today's date. Otherwise, type in the date when your readers will get the paper.

Step 3. Double click on the words Your City or Town. Type in the name of the city where you live. You can type in the name or your school instead if this is to be a school paper.

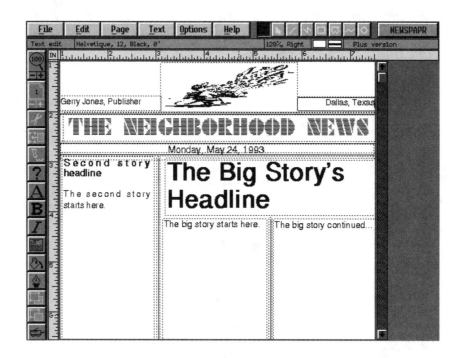

Step 4. (This step is optional. You don't have to do this, but you can if you want to.) The name of the newspaper on the template is *The Neighborhood News*. That's a pretty good title, but if you want to change the name of the paper, simply double click on the title and type your new title in the box. If your new title doesn't fit, use the Type Specs box you have used in other projects to make the words smaller or larger. You can also change the typeface if you want to. It's okay to experiment until you get exactly what you want.

That completes the basic masthead. Now you're ready to enter the news stories that you and your reporters have gathered.

ENTER AND PLACE THE NEWS STORIES

Just like the publisher of a big city newspaper, you need to decide where to put the stories. Deciding where to put the news stories takes a little bit of thinking. The most important stories should come first. The least important stories should go on the back pages.

The most important story is called the *lead story*. This story always goes on the first page. You need to decide which story will be the lead story in your paper.

Before you enter the lead story, however, you need to come up with a headline. Remember how you used a headline on the lawnmowing flyer project to get people's attention? You do the same in a newspaper. A headline is used to get attention so people will want to read the story.

Your biggest headline should tell people about the lead story. Good headlines have fewer than 10 words. That's about as many words as you can read with a quick glance. The bigger the headline, the more important the story. Look at the headlines in your local paper to learn more about them.

Here are examples of headlines that might be used in a neighborhood paper:

Garbage Truck Knocks Over Tree on Elm Street

The Braves Crush the Spartans 27 to 3

Summer Vacation Starts on Monday!

New Swimming Pool Opens at Sawyer Park

Kristy's Cat Has 6 Kittens!

Once you have decided on a headline and a lead story, add them to your newspaper by following the steps.

HOW TO ENTER THE HEADLINE AND LEAD STORY

Step 1. With the Text Tool, select the words from the template that say Main Headline Goes Here. Type in your new headline. If it won't fit in the text box, try to use fewer words.

This is the main headline.

Step 2. Now you can type in your lead story. There are two columns under the headline for the story. Your story should be long enough to fill both columns.

How Make Paragraphs with EnVision Publisher

To start a new paragraph with EnVision Publisher, press the Enter key at the end of the paragraph you just finished. Then, press the Tab key once. This will add an indent to the paragraph, as shown on the next page. Once you have pressed the Tab key, start typing the paragraph.

IF YOUR STORY IS TOO LONG...NOW WHAT?

If the story isn't finished when you reach the bottom of the first column, the words will disappear if you keep typing! There's a way to fix that, though. Here's how. Remember that you learned how to make a text box bigger in Chapter 4. You also know that you can get more words in a space by making the type smaller. Neither of these methods is appropriate for a newspaper, however. All newspaper stories should fit neatly in their columns and use the same size type. This makes the paper easier to read.

So, instead of changing the size of the typeface or making the columns wider, you can make a long story go to the next column if you tell EnVision to pick up the words that won't fit and move them. Here are the steps to make it work.

HOW TO PUT A STORY IN TWO COLUMNS

Step 1.   When you get near the bottom of the column, keep typing until a plus sign (+) appears at the bottom of the text box. You may not be able to see the last words you type. Don't worry. They're still there.

Step 2. Move the pointer to one of the + signs at the bottom of the box. It will turn into a tiny pair of scissors.

Step 3.   Click once with the scissors. An information box asks you, Cut overflowing text to clipboard? Click Yes. This grabs all of the text that wouldn't fit and puts it in a place inside the computer called the clipboard. The clipboard is a place for keeping type and pictures until you decide where to put them.

Step 4. With the Text Tool, click once on the next column, as shown, to select it. Click once more. The flashing line that appears means EnVision is ready for typing.

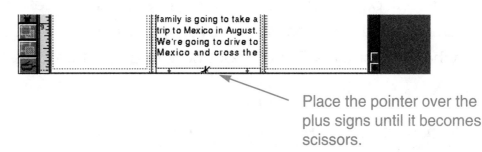

Place the pointer over the plus signs until it becomes scissors.

Step 5. Select Paste from the Edit pull-down menu. This tells EnVision to paste the words from the clipboard into the column. The extra type will appear instantly.

That's all there is to it! It doesn't matter if the column you add the extra type to is on the same page or on a different page of the newspaper. If you put the rest of the article on another page, however, you'll need to tell people where the story is. Read about how to do that on page 154.

THE SECOND FRONT PAGE STORY

Now that you've got your lead story entered, it's time to fill up the rest of the newspaper with news and features. The front page has enough room for a second story. This story should be shorter and slightly less important than your lead story.

TO PLACE YOUR SECOND STORY ON THE FIRST PAGE

Step 1. Select the words Headline for a Smaller Story by double clicking on the sentence with the Text Tool. (Remember to make the text box active by clicking on it once with the Text Tool.) Type in a short headline for the story.

Step 2. Double click on the sentence The second story starts here. Type in the second story.

When you're done, the first page should look something like this one.

Step 3. If there's not enough room for the second story in the column, follow the steps on page 145 to copy the extra words to the clipboard. Then, choose a column on page 3 or 4 and paste the words from the clipboard. Page 152 shows you how add *jumps* to your story. These are used so readers know where to finish reading the story. (If you are creating a one- or two-page newspaper, make your stories short enough to fit on page 1.)

That completes the front page of your newspaper! If you only want to make a one-page newspaper, skip to page 167 for help printing it.

THE INSIDE STORIES

The front page of the newspaper is special, because it's the page the reader sees first. The other pages are called *inside pages* because they're inside the newspaper. Readers don't see them until after they've read the first page.

The next step is to assemble the inside pages. We'll show you how to put together page 2. If you want to add more stories for pages 3 and 4, you will be able to complete these pages without the book's help. The steps are very similar to those for page 2, so you will already know what to do!

ON TO PAGE 2

Page 2 has room for a sports column, a weather column, and classified ads. These sections are standard in most newspapers, so you will probably want to include them in your paper.

The sports column might might be a good place to report on your school's games or describe a big game you watched on TV or attended with your friends.

HOW TO CREATE THE SPORTS COLUMN

Step 1. Double click on the word Headline with the Text Tool after clicking once to make the text box active. Type the headline for the sports column. If you want to write a story on something else, type the headline for that instead.

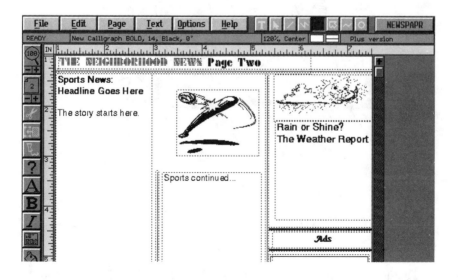

Step 2. Double click on the sentence The story starts here. Then type your story. If you want the story to go to another column on page 3 or 4, follow the steps that start on page 152.

RAIN OR SHINE?

Most newspapers have a weather report, and you can add one to your paper, too! Get the weather report from the radio, TV news, or from the city newspaper. If your paper will take a few days to finish, add the weather report last so that it is up to date. No one wants to read last week's weather!

Keep the weather section short and use a simple headline. Sunny with Temperatures into the 80s is enough for the headline. In the story, you can report on yesterday's weather, the forecast, or unusual weather conditions. If it's been an unusually hot summer or a very cold and snowy winter, write about it in the weather column.

To add the weather column to the newspaper, follow the same steps you used for entering other stories. Just select the words and type in the new information.

CONTINUED ON PAGE 795...

When a story begins on one page and ends on another, it is called a *jump*. If a story begins on page 1 and you paste the rest of the words into a column on page 3, you have jumped the story between pages. There's nothing wrong with jumping a story. Newspapers and magazines do it in every issue. But, you've got to let your readers know where to find the rest of the story!

Look for some jumps in your local paper. You'll see that the newspaper tells you where the rest of the story is. You must tell your readers where to look for the end of your stories as well. At the bottom of the first page of the story, you could add the words, Story continued on page 3. This tells your reader to look on page 3 to find the rest of the story. Then on page 3, you add the words, Story continued from page 1. Here are the steps so you can add these messages to your stories when you need to.

HOW TO ADD THE MESSAGES FOR STORY JUMPS

Step 1. Create a small text box with the Text Tool at the bottom of the first part of the story. Type in the words Story continued on page 3.

Step 2. Make the type into size 10 using the type controls. Place the text box at the bottom of the story. If you need to, make the text box containing the story a little smaller so you can fit the extra box.

It was Gerry Jones turn at the bat. She picked it up and took two steps forward to the plate. The pitcher wound up
Continued on Page 4

Step 3. Create a small text box on the page where the story is continued. Type Story continued from page 1. Place the box at the top of the story. If you need to, make the column with the story a little smaller to fit the extra box.

Continued from Page 2
up and threw. Gerry let her bat fly and missed. Strike 1, Mr. Cole our gym teacher yelled.

Do this for all stories that start on one page and finish on another page. If you do, your readers will have no trouble reading each story from start to finish.

SELLING AND CREATING ADS FOR YOUR NEWSPAPER

If you have something you want to sell, like an old bike or some toys you don't play with any more, you can advertise these in your paper. You can also sell advertising for your newspaper to people, stores, and businesses. People who want to sell things often advertise their products in the newspaper. They pay the publisher a fee to print their ads.

You have to decide how much to charge for the ads in your paper. Newspapers charge for ads based on their size. The bigger the ad, the more it costs. For example, an ad with three lines of information might cost 50 cents in your paper. A larger ad with a picture might cost a dollar or more. You can sell ads as tall as one column, 1/2 a column, 1/4 of a column, or less. You can even make an ad as big as a whole page of the newspaper. A one-page ad should be very expensive. If you're not sure what to charge for your ads, ask your parents or teacher to help you set a good price.

After determining the price of the ads in your paper,

you will need to ask your friends, family, and store owners if they have something they want to advertise. If they do, they will tell you what they want the ads to say and how big the ads should be. Have these people write a headline and the body copy for their ads on a piece of paper so you can correctly enter them in your newspaper.

The money you make from selling ads and subscriptions will help pay for the paper and supplies used to create your paper. The money left over from the ads and the subscriptions is the profit from the newspaper. You can spend the profit on things you want or you can save it in

Ads

Mountain Bike for Sale
Bright red mountain bike for sale. Like new. $75. Call Tim at 555-8888.

A sample ad for the ad section.

the bank to use later. For example, if you are creating the newspaper with your classmates at school, you might use the money earned from your paper to buy new uniforms for the school band or pay for a field trip to visit a museum or buy tickets to see a concert.

In the newspaper template there is a section for ads. If you don't want to include ads in the paper, you can simply delete the words and use the space for another news story.

If you want to include ads in your paper, the steps for making an ad are similar to those used to create the business flyer you created in Chapter 4.

HOW TO CREATE ADS FOR THE NEWSPAPER

Step 1. Draw a text box with the Pointer Tool to make the ad the correct size. (You can also make an existing text box smaller or larger to fit in the column.) An ad should always be at least as wide a column in the paper. The person or company paying for the ad will tell you exactly what the ad should say and how big it should be.

Step 2. Type in the headline for the ad. Make the headline big and bold by choosing a large type size in the Type information box and clicking on the Bold button (B) as you've done before for the headlines in cards and flyers.

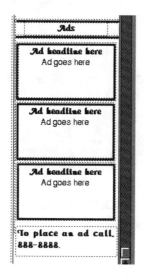

Step 3. The copy should describe the product or event. Make sure a phone number or address is included in the body copy as well. Make the body copy smaller than the headline. When you choose a type size, make sure all the words fit in the ad. Experiment with different type sizes to see what looks the best.

Step 4. Use the Box Tool to draw a frame around the ad. This will make the ad easier to find.

That's all there is to it. The ad is done. Of course, if an ad is very large, you can add pictures to it. Just follow the steps you used to add pictures to your flyers and cards in the other chapters.

Ads can promote a sale at a store, sell a product, or announce a special event such as a swim meet, soccer game, or school play. You will discover that it takes some work to sell the ads for your paper. However, if you are persistent at selling the ads, you'll be rewarded for your efforts by making some extra money.

PAGES 3, 4, AND MORE

You can add more stories and features to pages 3 and 4. Just follow the steps you learned in this chapter for adding type and jumping stories across columns and pages. You can also add more ads to these pages by following the steps you just learned.

ADDING MORE PAGES TO THE PAPER

If you run out of space in the four pages provided in the template, you will need to add more pages to your newspaper. To add more pages, go to the last page in the newspaper and then use EnVision's Insert... command in the Page pull-down menu. Type in the number of pages to add and EnVision will add them automatically, complete with the three text box columns in place.

Tell EnVision exactly how many pages you want to add to the paper.

Insert pages

Insert [4] page(s)

☐ Before   ■ After

Page: [4]

OK

Cancel

☑ Adjust objects to margins

This document has 1 page(s).

You will need to use the Line Tool to draw lines between the text box columns. Here are the steps to follow.

HOW TO ADD LINES TO THE COLUMNS OF A NEW PAGE

Step 1. Click on the Line Tool in the Toolbar. Click and drag between the columns toward the bottom of the page. As you move the mouse, a line will appear with an empty square on each end.

Step 2. Scroll to the bottom of the page and drag on the empty square at the bottom of the line until you reach the bottom of the column.

File	Edit	Page	Text	Options	Help		NEWSPAPR

Draw object | Helvetique, 12, Black, 0° | 120%, Center | Plus version

Add lines between the columns with the Line Tool.

Step 3. Add lines between all of the columns on all new pages in the same way.

To resize or move a line, you click on it once with the Pointer Tool. Two empty squares appear at each end. Drag one to change the length of the line. Click on it one more time, and a black square will appear at the middle. Drag it to move the line.

ADD MORE PICTURES TO THE PAPER IF YOU WANT TO

The template for the newspaper includes some pictures, but you may want to change these pictures or add other ones. You already know how to place pictures from the clip art that came with *The Create-It Kit*. If you get tired of using the same pictures, you can order more clip art from *The Create-It Kit* people or from the company that makes EnVision Publisher. There are addresses and coupons in the back of the book to order these.

You can also add pictures to EnVision Publisher publications and your newspaper from other sources. The only restriction is that all pictures must be saved as black-and-white (monochrome) or 16-color PCX files. If the file is in the correct format, it will have a .PCX at the end of the file-name. (If you aren't sure, ask an adult to make sure the art files are saved in the correct format. An experienced computer user can tell you what to look for.)

PAINTING PICTURES OF YOUR OWN

If you have almost any kind of painting program for your computer, you can paint your own pictures for your publications. There is one inexpensive painting program called NeoPaint that you can order from PCSig. We have included the address in the back of the book if you want to order this program. Remember to save your computer

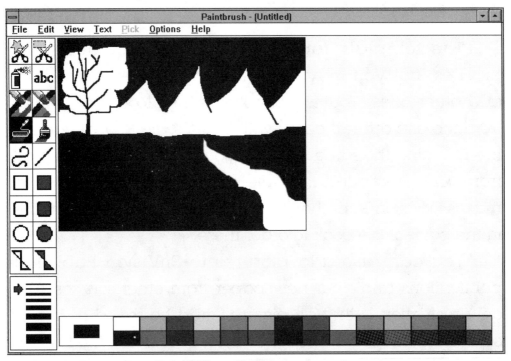

You can use almost any painting program to make your own pictures for use with EnVision Publisher. This is PC Paintbrush.

paintings in black-and-white or 16-color PCX format so you can import the picture into EnVision Publisher.

SCANNING PICTURES

If you have a scanner for your computer, you can scan family or school photographs and paste these into your EnVision publications. Have an adult show you how to operate the scanner if you've never used it before. If you don't have a scanner, you may be able to find a friend who does. Many schools now have scanners you can use. Again, save the scanned pictures as black-and-white or 16-color PCX format files so EnVision can import them.

FINDING OTHER PICTURES WITH ENVISION PUBLISHER

When you loaded clip art to make your flyer, you learned how to change to another directory on your computer's hard disk. This directory is where all the clip art from *The Create-It Kit* is kept. To import pictures from other places, you may need to move around on your computer's hard disk or use art stored on a floppy disk! Here's how to find the art stored on your computer.

If your clip art is kept in another place on disk, you may need to change to another directory. Directories are organized like a tree. The trunk of the tree is where you start out when you turn your computer on. (Remember when you typed CD \EVP? You were going up the tree to EnVision's branch. The command CD is short for Change Directory.) As you change directories, it's like you are moving up the main branches and then to the smaller branches and twigs of the tree.

EnVision is stored in one of the first main branches off the trunk. EnVision's clip art is stored in a smaller branch off the main branch containing EnVision. You may need to get clip art from another main branch off the trunk.

For example, if you use a paint program to create a picture of your own, you might save it in the same directory where the painting program is kept. To import the picture into EnVision, you would need to go down the trunk of the tree from the EnVision branch and back up the tree to the paint program's branch. You could then import the picture.

HOW TO CHANGE DIRECTORIES TO FIND THINGS

Step 1. To go to the trunk from EnVision's branch, in the Import information box, click once on the .. in the list of directories. This tells the computer to go down one branch to the tree's trunk.

Step 2. Click the Change Dir Button to go toward the trunk of the tree.

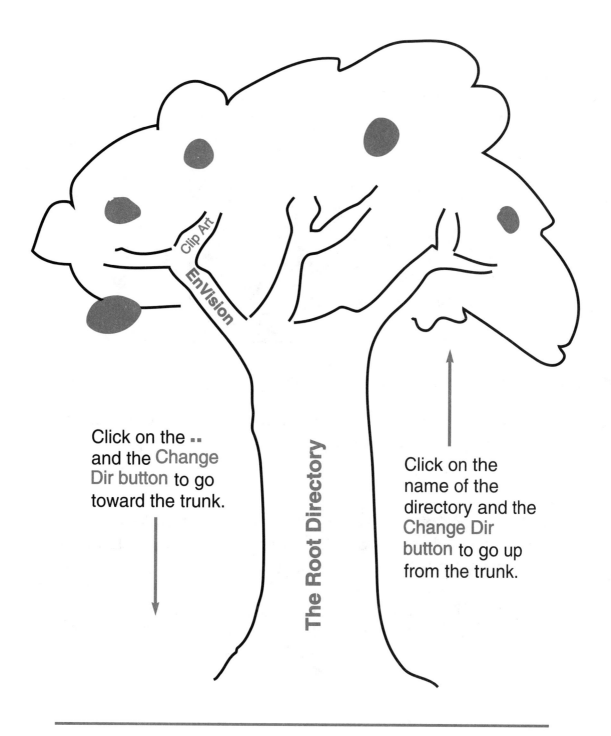

Clip Art

EnVision

Click on the **..**
and the Change
Dir button to go
toward the trunk.

The Root Directory

Click on the
name of the
directory and the
Change Dir
button to go up
from the trunk.

TO GO UP FROM THE TRUNK TO THE PAINT PROGRAM

Step 1. Click on the name of the directory of the paint program you see in the list of directories. Then click the Change Dir button.

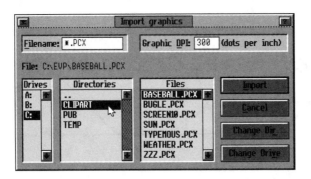

TO CHANGE TO ANOTHER DISK DRIVE

You may need to import clip art or scanned art from a floppy disk. You use the Import information box to do this. Here are the steps.

Step 1. Click on the letter of the drive you want to import a picture from. A: and B: are the letters for the floppy disk drives on most computers.

Step 2. Click the Change Drive button to change to the selected disk. If the picture is in a directory on the floppy disk, use the steps for moving up and down the directory tree to get to the right directory.

Step 3. After finding the directory where the picture is stored, click on the name of the picture in the Files box. If you can't find the picture there, just scroll through the Files box. When you find the picture you want to import, just click on the Import button as usual. The camera will appear on the page, and you can place your art wherever you want it by clicking on the page. Of course, you can always move the picture around or make it bigger or smaller. You already know how to do those things to pictures.

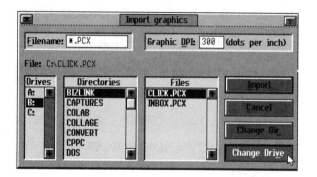

If you get the wrong picture on the page, just click on it once with the Pointer Tool and press the Delete key. Click Yes in the information box. This will delete the picture. Try the importing steps again until you get the picture you want.

GETTING THE PAPER READY FOR DISTRIBUTION

After you have all your stories, features, and pictures in place, your newspaper is ready to print. Before printing the copies for distribution, remember to check the entire paper to make sure there are no spelling errors or other mistakes.

You will print your newspaper on your computer's printer. You can print your paper on both sides of the same piece of paper the same way you printed the greeting card in Chapter 5. You can make as many copies as you need on the printer, but this might take a very long time if you have a lot of people who need to get the newspaper. Another way to make multiple copies is to print one copy of the paper and then have it photocopied at a store that offers copying services.

If your paper has 3 or 4 pages, you can tape the two pieces of paper together to make a single page, as shown on the next page. Then fold this page in half. A neater way to do this is to have your paper copied onto a single large piece of paper.

Have the newspaper copied on both sides of the big paper (11 inches by 17 inches). The copy store will be able to help you do this. Then fold the copy in half to create the finished newspaper. This looks really cool—just like a big daily newspaper!

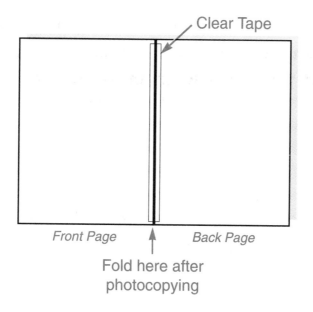

Clear Tape

Front Page

Back Page

Fold here after
photocopying

The final step in publishing a newspaper is to deliver your paper to the readers. A newspaper for your family can be given to Mom and Dad or mailed to relatives who live elsewhere. A neighborhood paper can be delivered to each house. Newspapers published at school can be put in boxes for classmates to pick up or you can ask your teacher to pass them out to the class.

Once you've delivered the paper, the job is done. But, now it's time to start work on the next edition! There's always more news to write about!

At this point, you have created some great projects and you've learned a lot of things about being a desktop publisher. But before you are ready to earn your certificate, there are still more neat things you should learn about

EnVision Publisher. In the next chapter you will learn some tricks you can do with colors, shapes, and sizes that you haven't tried yet. To see what fun lies ahead, just turn the page!

7. BE EVEN MORE CREATIVE— USE COLORS AND PATTERNS

You've learned to create all kinds of publications using EnVision Publisher. You're almost ready to earn your certificate as an Official Desktop Publisher. But there are a few more nick tricks you need to know about first. This chapter will show you a bunch of the best ones. Some of these tricks require a color printer, but most of them work with black-and-white printers.

Don't worry. You don't need a magic dragon to add special effects to your publications. There are better ways.

Before you read this chapter, get EnVision Publisher ready with a blank page. Then try the steps and play around. You'll be amazed at what you'll see.

WANT A MORE COLORFUL ENVISION PUBLISHER?

If you're working on a color monitor, choose Display colors... from under the Options pull-down menu. Click on the Rainbow button and click OK. This will turn EnVision's desktop into a rainbow of colors! You can try the other color combinations too. Experiment to see what you like best.

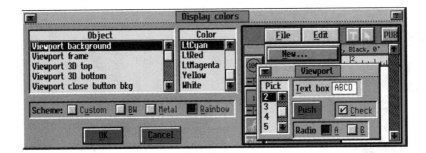

CHANGING LINES, TYPE, AND SHAPES

EnVision Publisher lets you change the shapes and patterns of lines, boxes, and letters. You can change the thickness or look of lines and the edges of shapes. You can also add patterns to letters, boxes, and circles. These patterns are called *fill patterns*. Fill patterns are a neat effect, though you shouldn't use them too often because they can make things difficult to read.

FILLING BOXES, CIRCLES, AND POLYGONS

To fill a shape before you draw it:

Step 1. Click on the Paint Bucket button. This will open the Fill Specs information box.

Click on the
Paint Bucket
button to open
the Fill Specs
information box.

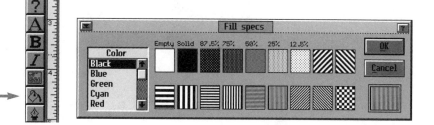

Fill box

Step 2. Amazing. Look at all the patterns you can choose. Click on one of the fill patterns. You'll see your selection in the window at the right of the box. Click OK.

Step 3. Click on the Box Tool, Circle Tool, or Polygon Tool in the Toolbar and draw a shape. Then, click twice on a blank part of the page so that the newly drawn shape is no longer active. EnVision will then draw it with your choice of fill pattern.

Now play around. Choose some fill patterns and then draw some shapes on the page.

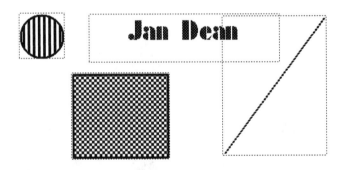

ADDING FILL PATTERNS TO TYPE

Type can also contain a fill pattern. You have to use this trick on very large type. Type that is too small will become hard to read if you add a pattern to it. But, for headlines and other big letters, patterns look pretty cool. In fact, the masthead of the newspaper *The Neighborhood News* was made up of type containing a fill pattern.

HOW TO CHANGE THE FILL PATTERN OF LETTERS

Step 1. Select your words with the Pointer Tool. Click on the A in the Control Bar. When the Type Specs information box appears, click the Use fill patterns button and click OK. The selected type will be filled with a pattern.

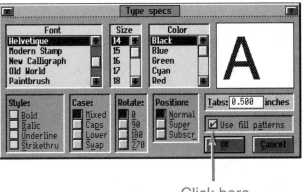

Click here
to used
filled type.

Step 2. To select another fill pattern, click on the Paint Bucket button in the Control Bar. This opens the Fill Specs information box. This box lets you choose another pattern.

Step 3. Click on the pattern you want to use. You will see it appear in the window at the right of the box. Click OK to see the pattern in the type. The type will be drawn with the pattern you select.

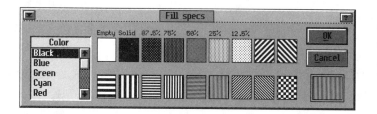

Click to change the fill pattern of your type.

CHANGING LINES AND SHAPE BORDERS

You can also change the way lines look. You can changes lines drawn with the Line Tool and also the lines that make up the edges of squares, circles, and any other shape drawn with EnVision. You must select the kind of line you want to use before drawing the line, box, circle, or other shape. Here's what to do.

HOW TO CHANGE THE WAY LINES LOOK

Step 1. Click on the Pen button in the Control Bar. This will open the Line information box.

Step 2. Click on the kind of line you want from the menu. There are thin lines, thick lines, and dotted lines. You'll see your selection in the window at the right of the box. Click OK.

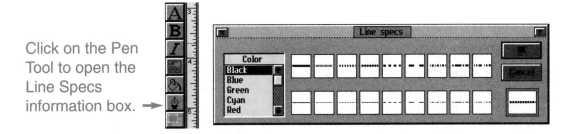

Click on the Pen
Tool to open the
Line Specs
information box. ➞

Step 3. Click on the Pen button in the Toolbar and draw a
line or shape. Now click twice on a blank part of the page so
that the newly drawn line or shape is no longer active.
EnVision will redraw the line as you requested.

ADDING COLOR TO TYPE, LINES, SQUARES, AND CIRCLES

You can always add color to your publications with
pens, crayons, and paints—but, if you have a color printer,
you can create signs, flyers, greeting cards, and
newspapers that print in color! Adding color to type, lines,
and shapes is easy. Color publications look exciting in print!

ADDING COLOR TO LETTERS AND WORDS

You can add color to words and letters through the
Type information box. To add a color, you select the words
you want to change and click on the A in the Control Bar.
This opens the Type information box. To choose a color:

Step 1. Drag the box in the list of colors until you see the color you want to use. EnVision offers 16 different colors, including black.

Step 2. Click on a color to select it. You will see the A in the window at the right side of the box take on the new color.

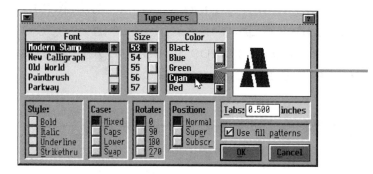

To color type, select it with the Text Tool and then choose a color here.

Step 3. Click OK and your type will instantly appear in color!

Remember, your words and pictures will only print in color if you have a color printer.

ADDING COLOR TO LINES AND FILLS

You can add color to lines and fill patterns by following the same steps for changing lines and adding fills. Once the Fill Specs information box or Line Specs information box is open, select a color. Then draw the line or shape. Once you click twice on a blank part of the page, EnVision will draw the line or shape in your choice of color.

To color a fill or line, pick the color in either the Fill Specs or Line Specs information boxes.

PRINTING IN COLOR

If you own a color printer and add color to your EnVision publications, you can print them in color. To do this, follow the standard steps for printing. You may need an adult's help picking the right printer.

Check with an adult before printing more than one copy of your publication. Some color printers use very expensive paper and ink, so you don't want to waste any of the supplies.

TURNING WORDS ON THEIR SIDES

One of the neatest tricks EnVision can do is to rotate type. You can turn type sideways or even upside down. It's easy to do! Just follow these steps.

HOW TO ROTATE WORDS AND LETTERS

Step 1. Select the words to rotate with the Text Tool.

Step 2. Open the Type Specs information box by clicking on the A in the Control Bar.

Step 3. Click on one of the Rotate buttons as shown and click OK. The selected words will be turned around or upside down!

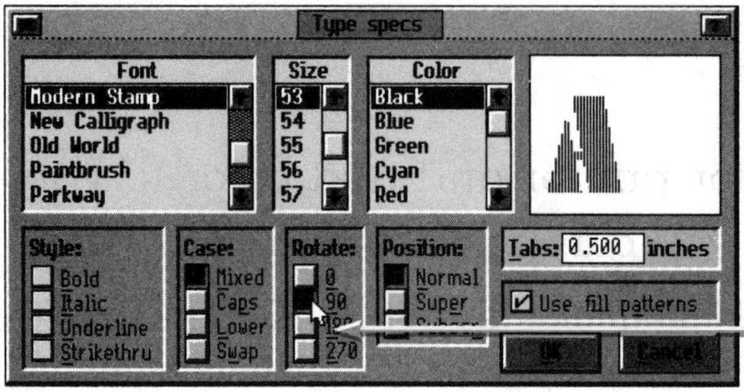

To rotate type, select it with the Text Tool and then click here.

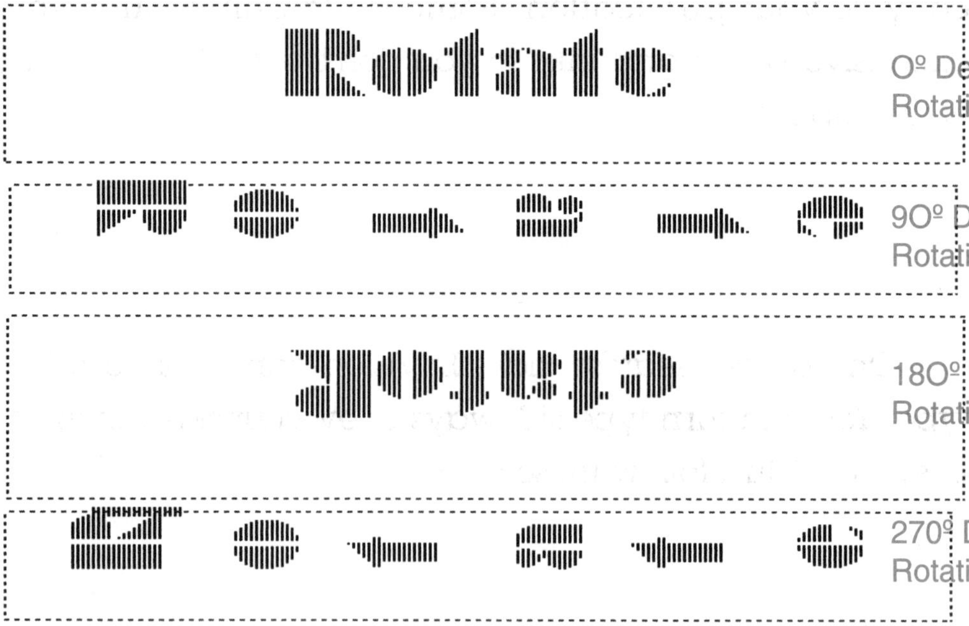

0º Degrees Rotation

90º Degrees Rotation

180º Degrees Rotation

270º Degrees Rotation

Well, that's about everything you need to know about EnVision Publisher to produce just about any kind of publication. You have done a good job and have earned your certificate as a Creative Desktop Publisher. In the next chapter, you'll learn how to print your certificate.

8. YOU'VE DONE IT—YOU'RE A REAL DESKTOP PUBLISHER!

Congratulations! You are now an expert desktop publisher! You know about typefaces, drawing, page layout, and printing. With the skills you learned in this book, you can make almost any kind of publication right on your own computer.

To prove that you've made it, your last project is to print a Certificate of Completion to verify that you are now a full-fledged desktop publisher.

To get your personalized Certificate of Completion, just follow these steps.

DO IT HOW TO FINISH THE CERTIFICATE OF COMPLETION

Step 1. Open the EnVision template called DIPLOMA.EVT.

Step 2. Select the words Your Name and type your name there instead.

Step 3. Type in today's date over the words Today's Date.

Step 4. Print your Certificate of Completion on your printer!

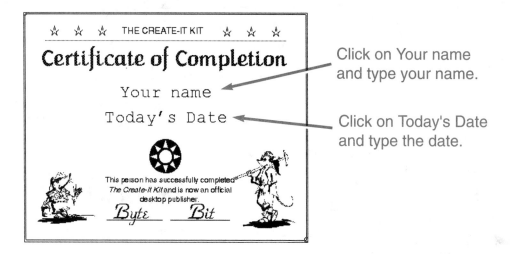

☆ ☆ ☆ THE CREATE-IT KIT ☆ ☆ ☆

Certificate of Completion

Your name

Today's Date

This person has successfully completed
The Create-It Kit and is now an official
desktop publisher.

Byte   *Bit*

Click on Your name
and type your name.

Click on Today's Date
and type the date.

That's it, you're now an official Create-It Kit graduate. You may want to mount your certificate on a piece of cardboard like you did with the sign you made in Chapter 3. Maybe your parents will want to buy a frame for your certificate. Once you've glued it to a piece or cardboard or framed it, hang the certificate proudly on a wall over your computer or in your room.

Now that you have learned about desktop publishing, you can continue to create publications whenever you want to. If you need a sign, flyer, or card, you'll be ready with your computer to create something personal and special. If you want to tell people the news, you can create your own newspaper. With your skills and EnVision Publisher, there are no limits. Make as many projects as you can. The more you publish, the more fun it gets.

By the way, Bit, Byte, and all their mouse friends have had a good time working with you. They told us that you're a pretty creative kid. We already knew that. Just look at all the creative things you've already done.

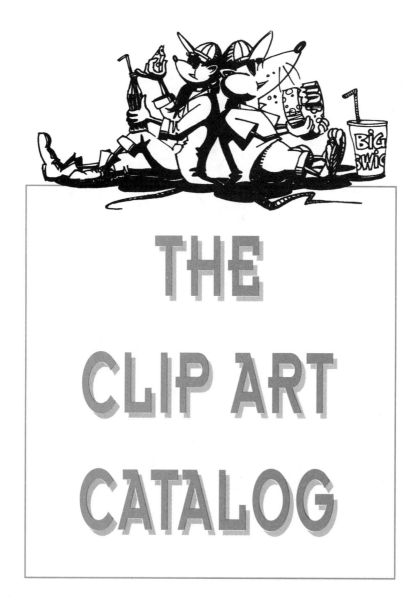

THE
CLIP ART
CATALOG

THE COMPLETE CREATE-IT KIT
CLIP ART CATALOG

This catalog displays all the clip art pictures provided on the disk that is packaged with *The Create-It Kit*. Each picture in the following catalog includes the name of the file so you can find it easily on your hard disk.

The pictures are installed automatically on your hard disk when you install EnVision Publisher. (The installation procedures for EnVision Publisher start on page 213.)

After EnVision Publisher is installed on your hard disk, any of the pictures can be used in any EnVision Publisher document. Just use the Import... command and type the name of the clip art file into the Import Information Box. Click OK.

The information box will disappear and a tiny camera will appear. Move the camera where you want the picture pasted and click once. This will paste the picture on the page.

Have fun with the pictures! Be creative. Use them together. Use them alone. Combine them on the same page. The pictures are yours to use over and over again!

Super Cool Easter Bunny

File Name
BUNNY.PCX

IDEAS FOR USING THIS PICTURE

- Easter card

- Easter party flyer

- Easter egg hunt

A Real Thanksgiving Turkey

File Name
TURKEY.PCX

IDEAS FOR USING THIS PICTURE

- Thanksgiving Day dinner invitation

- Thanksgiving cards

Leprechaun's Pot o' Gold

File Name
POTOGOLD.PCX

IDEAS FOR USING THIS PICTURE

- St. Patrick's Day card

- Contest flyer

Wacky Groundhog

File Name
GHOG.PCX

IDEAS FOR USING THIS PICTURE

- Groundhog Day newsletter

- Birthday card

Christmas Tree with Star Top

File Name
TREESTAR.PCX

IDEAS FOR USING THIS PICTURE

- Christmas cards

- Christmas gift tags

Santa's Jet Sleigh

File Name
SANTAJET.PCX

IDEAS FOR USING THIS PICTURE

- Christmas cards and party invitations

- Newsletter

Christmas Tree with Lots of Presents

File Name
TREEPRES.PCX

IDEAS FOR USING THIS PICTURE

- Christmas cards

- Christmas party with a gift exchange

Holiday Wreath

File Name
WREATH.PCX

IDEAS FOR USING THIS PICTURE

- Christmas gift tags

- Name cards for the table

Fireworks Bursting in Air

File Name

FIREWORK.PCX

IDEAS FOR USING THIS PICTURE

- Invitation to
  4th of July party

- Birthday card

- July newsletter

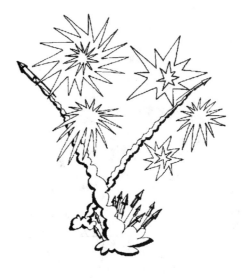

A Menorah

File Name

MENORAH.PCX

IDEAS FOR USING THIS PICTURE

- Jewish religious
  occasions and
  holidays

A Real *Scary* Halloween Mask

File Name
MASK.PCX

IDEAS FOR USING THIS PICTURE

- Invitation to a Halloween party

- A haunted house flyer

Blacky and the Pumpkin Brothers

File Name
BLACKY.PCX

IDEAS FOR USING THIS PICTURE

- Invitation to a Halloween party

- October newspaper

Halloween Witch and Hungry Helpers

File Name

WITCH.PCX

IDEAS FOR USING THIS PICTURE

- Halloween party invitations

- Halloween cards

- Newsletter

Birthday Party Fireworks

File Name

BDAYCAKE.PCX

IDEAS FOR USING THIS PICTURE

- Birthday cards

- Birthday party invitations

Big Bunch of Presents

File Name
PRESENTS.PCX

IDEAS FOR USING THIS PICTURE

- Birthday cards

- Birthday party invitations

Cool Birthday Party Bear

File Name
BDAYBEAR.PCX

IDEAS FOR USING THIS PICTURE

- Birthday cards

- Party invitations

Patriot's Game

File Name

OLDGLORY.PCX

IDEAS FOR USING THIS PICTURE

- President's Day

- Patriotic events

Happy Valentine's Day!

File Name

VALENTIN.PCX

IDEAS FOR USING THIS PICTURE

- Valentine's Day
  cards and
  presents

A New Sister or Brother

BABYNEWS.PCX

IDEAS FOR USING THIS PICTURE

- Card announcing a new member of the family

Dress-Up Party Invitation

File Name

TOPHAT.PCX

IDEAS FOR USING THIS PICTURE

- Invitation to a dress- up party or fancy affair

- Wedding cards

A Home Run!

File Name
HOMERUN.PCX

IDEAS FOR USING THIS PICTURE

- Invitation to your team's game or to watch a game on TV

- Sports column

Through the Hoop

File Name
BASKET.PCX

IDEAS FOR USING THIS PICTURE

- Invitation to your team's game or to watch a game on TV

- Sports column

SuperBowl XXX

File Name
FOOTBALL.PCX

IDEAS FOR USING THIS PICTURE

- Invitation to your team's game or to watch a game on TV

Top Gun

File Name
TOPGUN.PCX

IDEAS FOR USING THIS PICTURE

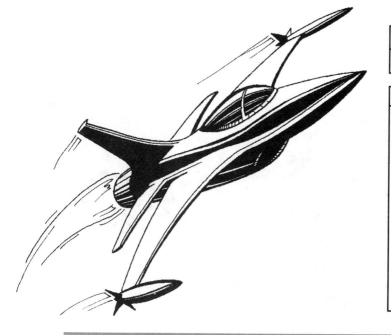

- Invitation to a paper airplane contest

- Articles on flying

News Around the World

File Name
VIDEO.PCX

IDEAS FOR USING THIS PICTURE

- Flyer for video taping business

- News column in a newspaper

- -

Hold On Fido!

File Name
DOGWALK.PCX

IDEAS FOR USING THIS PICTURE

- Flyer for dog walking business

- Birthday card

Computer Wizard

File Name

DTPMOUSE.PCX

IDEAS FOR USING THIS PICTURE

- Flyer for desktop publishing business

- Picture in a newspaper

Super Mower

File Name

LAWNMOW.PCX

IDEAS FOR USING THIS PICTURE

- Flyer for lawnmowing service

Cool Snow Shoveling Business

File Name
SNOWMAN.PCX

IDEAS FOR USING THIS PICTURE

- Flyer for snow shoveling business

- Winter party invitations

The Super Editor

File Name
TYPIST.PCX

IDEAS FOR USING THIS PICTURE

- Flyer for a typing business or a writing contest

- News column in a newspaper

School Play

File Name
COMEDY.PCX

IDEAS FOR USING THIS PICTURE

- Flyer announcing a school play

- Birthday card

Announcing!!!!!!!

File Name
ANNOUNCE.PCX

IDEAS FOR USING THIS PICTURE

- Flyer or card announcing almost any special event

A Burger and Fries to Go, Please...

File Name

HOTDOG.PCX

IDEAS FOR USING THIS PICTURE

- A picnic invitation

- A party announcement

Cool Stuff

File Name

ICECREAM.PCX

IDEAS FOR USING THIS PICTURE

- Birthday cards

- Invitations to an ice cream party

Jet Stream Jet

File Name

JET.PCX

IDEAS FOR USING THIS PICTURE

- Travel column in a newspaper

- Story about a plane trip

Ships At Sea

File Name

SHIPSSEA.PCX

IDEAS FOR USING THIS PICTURE

- Travel column in a newspaper

- Story about a boat trip

Big Goofy Dog

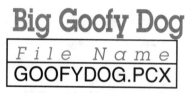

File Name
GOOFYDOG.PCX

IDEAS FOR USING THIS PICTURE

- Story about a dog

- Birthday card

Kittens

File Name
KITTENS.PCX

IDEAS FOR USING THIS PICTURE

- Story about some cats

- Birthday card

Another Cool Character

File Name
PENGUIN.PCX

IDEAS FOR USING THIS PICTURE

- Party invitation

- Winter dance flyer

A Star and the Moon

File Name
STARMOON.PCX

IDEAS FOR USING THIS PICTURE

- Birthday card

- Flyer for a night sports event

Prancing Unicorns

File Name

UNICORNS.PCX

IDEAS FOR USING THIS PICTURE

- Story about some unicorns

- Birthday card

The Big City

File Name

BIGCITY.PCX

IDEAS FOR USING THIS PICTURE

- Travel column in a newspaper

- Story about a trip to another city

Dinosaurs Going Places

File Name
DINO1.PCX

IDEAS FOR USING THIS PICTURE

- Story about dinosaurs

- Halloween party invitation

Dancing Dinosaurs

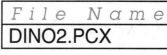

File Name
DINO2.PCX

IDEAS FOR USING THIS PICTURE

- Story about dinosaurs

- Halloween party invitation

Birthday Bash

File Name
BDAYBASH.PCX

IDEAS FOR USING THIS PICTURE

- Birthday card

- Birthday party invitation

Space Plane

File Name
SPACEPLN.PCX

IDEAS FOR USING THIS PICTURE

- Newspaper article

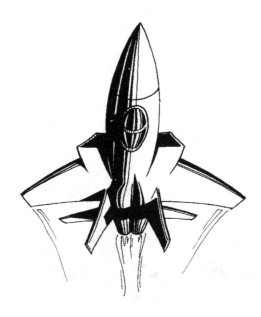

THE

BACK

PAGES

The Back Pages Contain These Sections:

- Installing EnVision Publisher on Your Computer
- For Adults: Computer Requirements and Printer Setup
- Suggestions for Parents and Teachers
- What to Do When Things Go Wrong
- About the Authors
- Even More Clip Art!
- Coupons for Ordering Clip Art and Fonts

INSTALLING ENVISION PUBLISHER ON YOUR COMPUTER

Before starting work with *The Create-It Kit*, you need to install EnVision Publisher and its files onto your computer's hard disk. Installing EnVision is easy because the program  does most of the work for you. All you need to do is to answer a few of questions and off you go!

If you have never installed a program on your computer before, or if you are using someone else's computer, make sure you have an adult available to help you with the installation.

 ## INSTALL IT NOW!

The steps for installing EnVision Publisher are simple. Here they are.

Step 1. Start your computer and let it wake up. This takes about 15 to 30 seconds.

Step 2. Put the disk that comes with *The Create-It Kit* into your computer's floppy disk drive. If your computer has two disk drives, use the slot that is the right size for the disk.

Step 3. If the floppy disk where EnVision is loaded is drive A, type A:. If your floppy disk is drive B, type B:. (Ask your adult helper if you don't know the letter used by the disk drive.) This switches control of your computer to the floppy disk that contains EnVision Publisher. Then type INSTALL.

Step 4. EnVision's installation program asks you to press Enter to install the program. Do so now.

Step 5. EnVision asks you the letter of the floppy drive where you inserted the disk. Type A or B as appropriate and press Enter.

```
═══════════ EnVision Publisher Plus v1.53 Installation ═══════════

  Please type the letter of the SOURCE disk drive (the disk drive where you
  inserted the EnVision Publisher diskette). This can be either A or B.

  Press ENTER when done, or ESC to cancel...




                              ┌───┐
                              │ B │
                              └───┘
```

Step 6. EnVision asks which drive is your hard drive. The answer to this question is usually C. Press Enter because C is already selected. (Ask your adult helper to make sure C is the correct choice. If not, your adult helper will know what to do.)

Step 7. Press Enter to create a directory called EVP where EnVision Publisher will be saved.

```
╔══════════ EnVision Publisher Plus v1.53 Installation ══════════╗

 Please enter the name of the directory on drive C where you wish to
 install EnVision Publisher, or press ENTER to accept the default EVP.
 To delete one character use BACKSPACE. To delete the whole line use DEL.

 Press ENTER when done, or ESC to cancel...


                        ┌─────────────┐
                        │ EVP         │
                        └─────────────┘
```

Step 8. : EnVision asks you to check the choices you've made for errors. If everything is correct, just press Enter.

NEXT PAGE☞

```
╔═══════════ EnVision Publisher Plus v1.53 Installation ═══════════╗

  You have selected:

    Source drive:       B
    Target drive:       C
    Target directory: EVP

  The installation program is now ready to start copying EnVision Publisher to
  your hard disk.

  Press ENTER to continue, or ESC to go back and change your entries...


╚══════════════════════════════════════════════════════════════════╝
```

EnVision now goes through an automatic loading sequence. This takes a few minutes while the program decompresses files and copies them to your hard disk.

Step 9. EnVision asks whether you want to load the clip art and templates. Type Y and press Enter. This takes a few minutes as well. Be patient. It's almost done.

```
╔═══════════ EnVision Publisher Plus v1.53 Installation ═══════════╗
  EnVision Publisher was installed on:

    Drive:     C
    Directory: EVP
    The clipart was installed in the subdirectory: EVP\CLIPART
    The templates were installed in the subdirectory: EVP\PUB

  You can now start EnVision Publisher by typing EVP.




╚══════════════════════════════════════════════════════════════════╝
```

That's all there is to it. The program is now ready for you to get creative.

FOR ADULTS: COMPUTER REQUIREMENTS AND PRINTER SETUP

EnVision Publisher and the files used in this book require about 2.9 MB of empty space on your computer's hard disk for installation. After installation is complete, the files require only about 2.5 MB of space. The program works with MS-DOS 2.0 and above and requires only 512K of memory for operation.

DISPLAYS

EnVision is compatible with almost all display formats. Read the sections titled "It Doesn't Work?" and "What Could Be Wrong?" later in this chapter for more information if you or your kids experience difficulties in using EnVision Publisher with your monitor.

MOUSES

EnVision Publisher fully supports the use of a mouse. If you have problems making your mouse work, read "It Doesn't Work?" and "What Could Be Wrong?" later in this chapter. EnVision Publisher can be run without a mouse, but we don't recommend it. Kids will quickly become frustrated with the slow pace of publication development without a mouse.

PRINTERS

EnVision supports a wide range of both color and black-and-white printers. It will work with PostScript printers although you may find that the wrong typefaces are substituted in PostScript mode. If this is a problem, you may want to temporarily disable your printer's PostScript cartridge or turn off Use PostScript Fonts in the Setup printer information box.

SETTING UP THE PRINTER

After loading EnVision Publisher, the printer needs to be set up for the program. EnVision can print to almost any model or brand of printer.

There are two steps to getting a printer ready. First, choose the brand and model printer. Then, pick an emulation mode. For example, some printers can be set up to run normally or, if they are equipped with a PostScript card, they can be set up to run in PostScript. (If you aren't familiar with PostScript, just follow the steps below and things should work fine.)

HOW TO SELECT THE PRINTER FOR ENVISION PUBLISHER

Step 1. Start EnVision Publisher. Click on the Print button at the lower left corner of EnVision's screen with the mouse. This opens the Print information box.

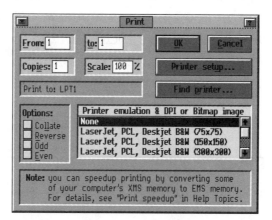

Step 2. Click on the Find Printer button with the mouse. This opens the Find Printer information box.

Step 3. Use the Scroll Bar to scroll through the list of printers to find the correct one. Once found, click once on it to select it and then click the OK button. (If you are using an older or unpopular dot-matrix printer that's not on the list, choose one of the Epson printers. For unlisted laser printers, choose any Hewlett Packard laser printer such as the HP LaserJet II.)

CHOOSE THE PRINTER EMULATION IF NECESSARY

Once a printer is selected, you may see several options appear in the bottom half of the Find Printer information box. Select the one that best matches the printer by clicking on one of the buttons.

For example, after selecting the Samsung Finale 8000 as the printer, three emulation modes appear. Choose the one that best fits the printer's setup such as PostScript B&W. Ask your computer dealer if you aren't sure what choice to make.

SETTING UP FOR SERIAL PRINTERS

While almost all modern printers are parallel, if you are running a serial printer, click on the Printer Setup button to set the parameters for your printer. Set the Port to whichever port your printer is plugged into. Set the other settings as indicated in the printer's manual. For most printers, leave the settings the way they were when you opened the box. Make sure Use PostScript fonts is left unchecked. Click OK when you're done.

That's all there is to getting EnVision Publisher ready to print. If printing problems are encountered, read the troubleshooting suggestions in the section titled "Advice for Adult Helpers—What to do if Things Don't Work as Expected."

SUGGESTIONS FOR PARENTS AND TEACHERS

The Create-It Kit includes EnVision Publisher on the bound-in disk with this book. This program was selected especially for *The Create-It Kit* because it is a powerful desktop publishing program that is also easy to learn and use. Any kid who can read can easily master the basics in a few hours. EnVision Publisher is also an excellent program for adults who are new to computers and desktop publishing. The program is not limited to kid's projects—it can be used to create a wide range of adult-oriented publications as well.

It is important for parents and teachers to know that EnVision Publisher is NOT a children's program. Admittedly, EnVision Publisher is a bit simpler than PageMaker or QuarkXPress (the two most widely used professional desktop publishing programs), but it is a real desktop publishing program. It is not a toy.

The skills and projects in *The Create-It Kit* may seem like fun, but the book has been carefully constructed to teach children *real* desktop publishing skills. The basic skills learned while creating the projects in this book can be applied to all of the major desktop publishing programs on the market today.

Good News for Educators with Limited Budgets— The Create-It Kit Runs on Older IBM Compatibles and New PCs Too!

EnVision Publisher and *The Create-It Kit* are compatible with not only the newest IBM compatible computers but also older machines running early versions of DOS. EnVision runs on older black and white or color display adapters too. Almost any kind of printer is compatible. This makes it possible for schools with older equipment to still teach children the latest in desktop publishing techniques.

If you want to buy multiple copies of *The Create-It Kit* for use in your school, contact Random House Electronic Publishing at 212/872-8030 and ask about educator's discounts.

The desktop publishing skills that will be mastered by children who create their own projects using this program include the use of typefaces, the specification of margins and page templates, the use of computerized drawing tools, the steps for importing graphics, and the use of special styles and fill patterns to add interest to publications.

We wanted the book to be both fun and educational. Teachers will find that each chapter in the book provides historical background and other information to bring the publishing projects to life. These short introductions could be expanded in the classroom to become complete studies of each of the areas presented in the book. For example, the first chapter introduces the history of publishing. This could be expanded into an in-depth study of books and publishing. The third chapter talks about signs and typography—a perfect opportunity to get students excited about observing the written communications in their everyday environment.

Beyond simply teaching the basic desktop publishing skills and striving to get kids interested in both computers and language, the chapters and projects can be adapted to a wide range of lesson plans and topics. *The Create-It Kit* provides a flexible vehicle for encouraging creativity and integrating language arts, computer skills, and other academic subjects.

For parents, *The Create-It Kit* provides an opportunity to get together with the kids to learn something new and create fun projects of practical value. We recommend that you work through some of the projects in *The Create-It Kit* as a family at night, on weekends, or when the weather is too bad to go outside and play.

The Create-It Kit has been written so kids can follow the instructions on their own. However, there are some times when the help of a parent, teacher, or adult friend are recommended. We suggest that an adult be available to help children who lack previous computer experience. It is also appropriate to assist children during the software installation process. Other than that, kids who can read can do most of the projects without much help from you. Of course, even if they can do most of the projects on their own, it is still important that you be actively aware of their desktop publishing activities and provide positive reinforcement for their work.

WHAT TO DO WHEN THINGS GO WRONG

There are times when kids might get stuck or when adults need additional information to help kids finish a publication. If you need to help someone answer a question about using a certain command in EnVision Publisher, there is a Help button on the Control Bar. The Help button looks like a question mark. Just click on the button and it will bring up a menu of topics to choose from. (Parents and teachers: Please note that some of the terms used in the help menus are different than the terms used in the book. We have tried to simplify the command names to be more accessible to children. As an adult, you shouldn't have any trouble matching the technical terms to the friendlier terms in *The Create-It Kit*.)

Most of the features in EnVision Publisher are covered in this book. However, there are a few advanced topics, such as style sheets and kerning, that have not been introduced. If you want to learn about these EnVision Publisher features, you can read about them in the Help menus. If you need more information than is provided in the Help menus, we recommend purchasing the *EnVision Publisher User's Guide* from Software Vision Corporation. There is an order form for the User's Guide at the end of the book.

TECHNICAL SUPPORT FOR ENVISION PUBLISHER

Free technical support is available from Software Vision Corporation, the developers of EnVision Publisher. Only parents, teachers, or children with adult supervision should call for technical advice. The technical support number is (813) 545-4354

If you experience problems, please read the questions and answers section that follows. If no solution is found, before you call for help, please note the manufacturer and model of your computer, the type of video display adapter installed in your computer, and the model of your printer. The support personnel at Software Vision will need to know about your hardware before they can resolve technical problems.

THE CREATE-IT KIT AND MICROSOFT WINDOWS—WHAT TO DO IF THE SCREEN LOOKS FUNNY

We recommend in Chapter 2 that kids access EnVision Publisher through MS-DOS instead of Windows because we want to make the loading as easy as possible. Many young readers may not understand much about computers, and Windows requires additional explanation that would waste pages of this book. You can run EnVision Publisher using the Windows MS DOS shell function.

If, however, you are using Windows and the shell function to run EnVision Publisher and the screen appears in fractured tiles, type Alt-F and then x to exit. Quit Windows and access the program directly from MS-DOS.

COMMON PROBLEMS AND HOW TO FIX THEM

Here are a few more solutions to problems that you or your child may experience when working through the projects in *The Create-It Kit*. Most of these problems are simple procedural or set-up errors that the instructions in this section can quickly resolve.

Q. Why are changes to type formatting not taking effect?

A. There are two possible reasons why changes in the Type

Specs information box or Type pull-down menu are not working. They are:

▪ The Text Tool has not been used to select the text. Do this by clicking once on the text box to make it active and then double clicking on words or sentences or by dragging across the text after the box is active. Once selected, you can make desired changes.

This text is not selected

▪ You must reselect text with the Text Tool each time you want to enter formatting information in the Text Specs information box. A blinking cursor between letters or at the start or end of a word means that text is no longer selected. Remember to select the text first before opening the Text Specs information box.

Q. Where are the templates? They don't show up in the Open information box.

A. In the Open information box, click on the Template button to see a list of templates.

Q. Why can't we finish drawing a polygon, squiggle, or zigzag line? It just keeps drawing after each double click.

A. You need to double click faster to tell EnVision to stop drawing.

Q. Why does the clip art look different in the Clip Art Catalog than it does on screen and in print?

A. We had to reduce the size of most of the clip art to make it fit the catalog. You can resize or change the shape of clip art using the Pointer Tool. Click once on the imported art to make it active. Then drag on any of the four black squares that appear at the corners of the art to resize or reshape the picture. (Remember that the fifth square in the center is used to move the image, *not* to resize it.)

Q. My mouse doesn't work. My mouse works with Windows but not EnVision Publisher. What's wrong?

A. You need to load your mouse driver and make changes to the AUTOEXEC.BAT and/or CONFIG.SYS files so that EnVision can see what the mouse is doing. The manual that came with your mouse will tell you what to do. Restart your computer after making changes to the files. (Very old mouses may require new software from the mouse's manufacturer to run with VGA display adapters. If you can't locate the company, consider purchasing an inexpensive new mouse for your system because you will have this problem with other software programs as well.) Stores such as Egghead Software can sell you a new mouse with the right software starting at $25. There is a cute mouse just for kids from LogiTech called The Kid's Mouse that looks like a real mouse! (Egghead sells it at this writing for $41.95.)

Q. Why are the wrong typefaces displayed in the printed publication? Why do they not print exactly like on screen?

A. Most likely you are using a PostScript or PostScript-compatible printer and the printer is substituting its fonts for EnVision Publisher's fonts. Turn off Use PostScript fonts in the Printer Setup information box. (Open the Print information box and click the Printer Setup button to make the changes.)

   An even better solution is to turn off the printer's PostScript function at the printer while printing from

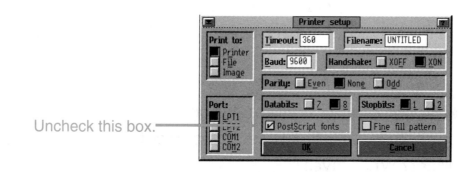

Uncheck this box.

EnVision. (See the printer's manual for help.) Then, select the correct printer from EnVision's list of printers and printer emulation options.

Q. My PostScript printer never prints anything, but the lights show that it is working, and EnVision seems to be trying to print.

A. There are two situations that may cause this problem. Make sure that you have selected PostScript as the emulation option or EnVision may think that it's printing to a non-PostScript laser printer. To fix this, choose PostScript as the emulation mode in the Print information box. Turn your printer on and off again to reset it before trying to print again.

If your document contains lots of pictures and fonts, it may take several minutes or more to print. Give EnVision more time before assuming there's a problem. PostScript printing, especially on older, slower printers often takes a long time. Again, consider switching off PostScript on your printer. This significantly speeds printing with EnVision Publisher.

Q. My printer won't print a full page. Or, my printer seems to hang and I've got it set up correctly with EnVision Publisher? What gives?

A. Your printer may need more memory. To print a full page with a desktop publishing program, the printer must be able to "remember" the entire page at one time. Your printer (not the computer) should have at least 1 to 1.5MB of memory. PostScript printing requires at least 2MB of memory or PostScript won't load on most printers.

Q. My dot matrix printer prints garbage. Or, my dot matrix printer stretches a document across more than one page. What is wrong?

A. Make sure you have picked the right printer and emulation mode. See the section on Page 218 on setting up your printer. If you pick the wrong printer, EnVision will transmit your publication incorrectly to your printer.

Q. What if EnVision doesn't display correctly on my monitor?

A. You can force EnVision into a monitor mode by starting it with a special command called a switch. For example, typing EVP CGA to start EnVision will force it to display in black and white regardless of the monitor you are using. Other supported switches include:

EVP VGA - Standard VGA

EVP EGA - Extended Graphic Adapter

EVP HERC - Hercules monochrome

ATT - ATT 640 X 400 mode

EVP SAFEVIDEO - For problems with older video cards, try this switch which turns off the direct video technique normally used by EnVision to speed display.

Q. Why are the names of some commands and functions different in the Help menu and in the optional manual?

A. We have tried to use simpler names for some functions because EnVision Publisher was originally created for adults. Because this book is intended for readers as young as six- or seven-years-old, we chose names for the commands and functions in EnVision Publisher that would be more fun and understandable for kids.

ABOUT THE AUTHORS

Sunny Baker

**Kim Baker
(note the beard)**

KRISTY JO

Kim and Sunny Baker are authors, business consultants, and desktop publishing experts who live in Tempe, Arizona. Sunny is also a college teacher. Kim is also an artist. They have written advanced books on desktop publishing including, Color Publishing on the Macintosh and Color Publishing on the PC.

This portrait of the authors was drawn by their niece, Kristy Jo Staron, who is almost six. Since she was the inspiration for this book, Kim and Sunny couldn't refuse when she wanted to draw their portraits for this page. The authors tested many of the projects in the book with Kristy Jo, who was always ready to provide advice on the things kids like to create.

EVEN MORE CLIP ART!

You can order more clip art with the coupons provided on the next pages. You can also get more clip art to use with EnVision Publisher from other places such as CompuServe. CompuServe is a company that you can call from your computer using a communications device called a modem. CompuServe has massive libraries of clip art. Have an adult help you use CompuServe. You will need a modem and there is a charge for using this service. You will need to get a conversion program such as GIF Converter which is also available on CompuServe. This shareware program is used to convert the clip art from CompuServe's GIF format to PCX format. Call 800/848-8199 to get a starter kit from CompuServe. This 800 number is good in both the U.S. and Canada.

Many local electronic computer bulletin boards offer free clip art. Again, you will need a modem to use the electronic bulletin boards. To find local bulletin boards look in your city's free computer newspaper. Call a computer store to find out the name of this publication and where you can find a copy. If there is no such publication in your area, ask a computer store about local bulletin boards.

Many software stores such as Egghead Software sell inexpensive clip art libraries as well. You can look in the back of almost any computer magazine for clip art sources.

Get more *Create-It Kit* clip art and templates!

For $19.95 you can get a disk of dozens of fun images by John Wincek, the book's illustrator. The disk also comes with five new templates.

You can use the clip art pictures and templates for invitations, cards, games, signs, stories, newspapers, flyers, or anything else you want to create.

The disk includes pictures of animals, buildings, vehicles, space ships, plants, sports, landscapes, people, and much more! Of course, pictures of Bit and Byte are also included.

Please send me more Create-It Kit Clip Art!

Yes, I would like more *Create-It Kit* clip art. I have enclosed a check or money order for $19.95 plus $2.00 shipping and handling. Send a check for the total of $21.95.

My computer uses: ❏ DOUBLE DENSITY disks.

❏ HIGH DENSITY disks.

Name _____

Address _____

City/State/Zip _____

School/Organization _____

Please mail this coupon and the check to:
Baker & Baker
2051 S. Dobson Rd., Suite 17375
Mesa, AZ 85202

Bit and Byte Ask You to Please Note:
A photocopy of the clip art coupon will work just fine for ordering, especially if this copy of the book belongs to someone else, like your friend, teacher, or the library. So please don't tear up somebody else's book. Make a copy!

3 Great Reasons Why You Should Mail This Registration Card

1. FREE 30-day telephone support. If you have a question about EnVision Publisher, you can call our technical support experts who are ready to guide you along.

2. FREE Quarterly EnVision Publisher Newsletter. The newsletter comes loaded with the latest news, tips, and tricks - direct from the creators of EnVision Publisher. It will also notify you of when new versions of EnVision Publisher become available.

3. LARGE discounts on other Software Vision products.

☐ **YES,** I want to become a registered user of EnVision Publisher, and enjoy the FREE benefits listed above. Here is my address:

Name:_____

Address:_____

City, State, Zip:_____

Telephone No:_____ Disk Size: ☐ 3.5" or ☐ 5.25"

Also, in addition to the Free benefits, I would like to buy some of the other Software Vision products checked below:

☐ **EnVision Publisher Manual:** *the original 300 page User's Guide.* **$10.**
☐ **Fonts Bash:** *23 fonts for your EnVision Publisher.* **$19.**
☐ **Clipart Bash:** *74 clipart images for EnVision Publisher.* **$19.**
☐ **Upgrade to EnVision Publisher Plus:** *300-page manual, 40 clipart images, 17 fonts, 8 templates, and current version of EnVision Publisher Plus.* **$29.**
☐ **Upgrade to EnVision Publisher Pro:** *300-page manual, 74 clipart images, 31 fonts, 13 templates, and current version of EnVision Publisher Pro.* **$69.**

Payment Method: ☐ Check Enclosed ☐ Money Order ☐ Visa ☐ MasterCard

Card Number: _____ Exp. Date: _____

Name on Card:_____ Signature:_____

Total of Order: $_____ Please include $3 for shipping charges.

Make checks payable to: Software Vision Corporation. Florida residents please add 7% sales tax to the order amount. Thank You for your order.

Mail to: Software Vision Corporation, P.O. Box 1734, Pinellas Park, FL 34664-1734, or **Call: 1-800-388-8474 or 813-545-4354. Fax: 813-541-5616.**

Cut along the dotted line and fold in half

Cut along the dotted line and fold in half

Please fold along this line

NO POSTAGE
NECESSARY
IF MAILED
IN THE
UNITED STATES

BUSINESS REPLY MAIL

FIRST CLASS MAIL PERMIT NO. 222 PINELLAS PARK, FLORIDA

POSTAGE WILL BE PAID BY ADDRESSEE

SOFTWARE VISION CORPORATION
PO BOX 1734
PINELLAS PARK FL 34664-9915

Software Vision License Agreement

This is a legal agreement between you (the licensee), and Software Vision Corporation ("Software Vision"). By using this program, you are agreeing to the terms of this agreement.

EnVision Publisher is protected by the United States Copyright law and international treaty provision, and therefore must be treated like any other copyrighted material. It is illegal to copy or reproduce EnVision Publisher or its documentation, with this exception: you are authorized to make one (1) archival copy of the EnVision Publisher disks for the sole purpose of backing-up our software and protecting your investment from loss. You must retain all such archival copies in your possession.

Software Vision grants you permission for the use of EnVision Publisher on a single computer. Any number or people may use EnVision Publisher and it may be freely moved from one computer location to another, so long as there is no possibility of it being used at one location where it is being used at another, unless, of course, our copyright has been violated. (If you must obtain a separate license for each user; please contact us for site license information.)

Updates

If the EnVision Publisher registration card has not been received by Software Vision, Software Vision is under no obligation to make any program updates available to you.